LET IT BE A DANCE

LET IT BE A DANCE

▼

My Life Story

Frank M. Calabria

Writers Club Press
San Jose New York Lincoln Shanghai

Let It Be A Dance
My Life Story

Writers Club Press
an imprint of iUniverse.com, Inc.

For information address:
iUniverse.com, Inc.
5220 S 16th, Ste. 200
Lincoln, NE 68512
www.iuniverse.com

Cover Photo of Frank and Angela Calabria by Mayela Calabria Harris

ISBN: 0-595-15339-9

Printed in the United States of America

DEDICATION

Dedicated to all my teachers, in and out of the classroom: my parents, my wife, our children and grandchildren, my friends and the many others who helped me create a life worth living.

PREFACE

The pearl is the oyster's autobiography.

Federico Fellini

When I began working on this autobiography, my intent was to entertain my family and friends and to reveal little-known information about myself. I also wanted to tell stories that might otherwise be forgotten: stories about my mother and her Gothic romances before she emigrated to America; stories about my grandfather, a "piece of work"; stories about my indoctrination into Catholicism when, as an altar boy, I sinned every other day (which required frequent trips to the Confessional); and stories about how I survived growing up a second-generation, Italian-American, in Brooklyn, with a large clan of relatives. A final compelling reason for telling my life story—since I am not famous, rich or powerful—if I do not tell my story, who will?

In the process of putting my life down on paper, I realized things about myself that I had not been aware of, and uncovered a common thread that runs through my existence. Who would have imagined that being confined to a wheelchair for a year in my boyhood would have had such an impact on the direction of my life? That year in a wheelchair led to my forming a body-building club, which gave me my first taste of teaching. Drafted into the service at age 18, I was assigned the job of physical training instructor. On weekends, I taught ballroom dancing at the local U.S.O. It was at that point that I realized two great passions in my life—ballroom dancing, which to this day brings me much joy, and teaching, which became my vocation. During a short stint as a salesman after my discharge, I became fascinated by human behavior and realized my third passion—psychology. One night while teaching ballroom dancing to pay for my graduate classes in psychology, I discovered my fourth passion—Angela, the girl of my dreams. We married, raised four wonderful children (and now have seven equally wonderful grandchildren). I became a professor of psychology and later opened a private practice in psychotherapy. What a fortuitous series of events!

I hesitate to speak too loudly of my good fortune for fear that some crone from the old country, upon hearing my good news, will cast the "mal occhio," the "evil eye", in my direction

Some say that moments before we die, our entire life flashes before our eyes. While this may be true, I prefer a more leisurely pace to review my life. Through writing this autobiography, I have savored it. Through reading it, I hope that you will too!

ACKNOWLEDGEMENTS

My gratitude to Patrick Kurp for editing an early version of my manuscript and giving me valuable feedback about the book's focus. My mother, Rosina Calabria, and my godmother, Lydia Ingellis, were two main sources of information about the family tree and what was happening during the early years. Argie Serras, in our frequent conversations, gave me both encouragement and insight into what my life was all about. Margaret Wadhera, my former editor, sharpened my focus in rewriting. Tommy Thompson and Alex Levy provided invaluable technical assistance.

My gratitude to my wife who, in reading over the various revisions, forced me to be lucid and honest. My greatest thanks go to my editor, Michelle Gabriella Belill, whose untiring efforts, well beyond the call of duty, enabled me to bring this manuscript to completion.

CHAPTER ONE

▼

IMMIGRANTS FORSAKING THE OLD WAYS FOR THE NEW

Whoever forsakes the old ways for the new knows what he is losing but not what he will find.

Italian proverb

It startles me to think that all people who came to settle in America, including the Indians and Eskimos, were foreigners, like my parents. My father and later my mother, were part of a wave of 5,000,000 Italians who emigrated to the United States between 1880 and 1920. From my mother's stories, and from other accounts I have read, coming to America was an ordeal. I can only marvel at the courage possessed by my parents and all those who emigrated from distant places in search of a better life.

My father and mother brought with them few valuable possessions. What they did bring, however, that was priceless was their "Italian Soul." Through their stories about where they grew up, how they met and married, how they built their home in America, and how they raised their children, I catch glimpses of the imprint they left upon my "Italian-American Soul."

My mother was born in the small town of Santa Sophia d'Epiro; my father came from the nearby town of Fuscaldo, both located in the province of Calabria, inland from the Mediterranean Sea. This section of Italy can best be imagined as the instep and toe of the Italian boot.

Calabria is one of six provinces which comprise the Mezzogiorno. Not having traced my father's genealogy, I don't know how it came about that his surname bears the name of this province. According to estimates by the United States Census Bureau, there are approximately 960 people in the United States carrying the Calabria name. With this surname, I cannot escape my Italian heritage—and who would want to? At least, I can't be lost among a throng of people who go by the names Smith or Jones.

The region of Calabria where both parents lived is called Magna Graecia, "Great Greece", founded around 770 B.C. In the November 1994 issue of *The National Geographic*, in an article which focuses on this region of southern Italy, the writer speculates that, perhaps, the first fires of democracy were fueled here before this political idea reached Athens.

In guide books, Magna Graecia is also known as The Mezzogiorno, *The Land of the Midday.* For most of its long history, this southern region of Italy has been referred to as "the land that time forgot." It is a part of Italy that has had more than its share of misery. In 1908, a major earthquake and tidal wave in Reggio, Calabria, destroyed the city; 20,000 people died. The government in the north, ever caught up in bureaucracy, was ineffective in dealing with this catastrophe and others that blighted the south.

Magna Graecia is a territory with a checkered history. Multiple cultures have succeeded one another in great variety: Byzantine, Norman, Jewish, Moorish, Albanian, Greek, Spanish and French. Douglas notes that despite the changing cultures, there has been little change in the landscape, which remains to this day pristine.

Norman Douglas, a scholar-traveler and gentleman-adventurer who toured this region, wrote about his travels in his book, *Old Calabria.* He describes this region, which dates back thirty-five centuries, as a land of tenacious antiquity. He documents the rich tradition of a country which blends paganism and Christianity, a place where stories of dragons and gods and goddesses are intermixed with those of flying monks. He identifies a religious tradition that venerates the Virgin Mother and relates that there are 2,000 subspecies of Madonna worship in different parts of southern Italy.

In his research, Douglas found the story of Saint Joseph of Copertino, affectionately known as "The Flying Monk," who was born on Sept. 18, 1663. This date precedes my birthday by five days and three centuries. An early prototype of Superman, Saint Copertino, in one of his most remarkable flights, "(detached) himself in the swiftest manner from the altar with a cry of thunder, he went, like lightning, gyrating hither and thither about the chapel and with such an impetus that he made all the cells of the dormitory tremble, so that the monks cried, 'An earthquake! An earthquake!'"

Even as a grown man, "The Flying Monk" would speak in childlike veneration to the Mother of God, addressing her as "La Mamma Mia." The mere pronouncement of her name was often sufficient to raise him from the ground into the air. Saint Copertino performed a variety of miracles even Superman could not perform, like multiplying bread and wine, calming a tempest, driving out devils, causing the lame to walk and the blind to see. All of these miraculous feats, according to Douglas, were duly attested by eye-witnesses under oath.

When I compare the relatively brief history of America with the ancient history of Calabria, my parents can justly claim pride in a long and varied inheritance. But I must be quite up front about the status of my parents. My mother made it clear to me that while she did not come from an upper-class family, it wasn't lower-class either. Both my grandfathers were skilled craftsmen whose families never went without. However humble their origins, I like to entertain the fantasy that I am descended from royal lineage.

Such childhood imaginings were reinforced in Douglas' book, where he quotes the learned Aceti who describes Calabria as "a land of great men." Aceti, in 1737, "…was able to enumerate over two thousand celebrated Calabrians, athletes, generals, musicians, centenarians, inventors, martyrs, ten popes, ten kings, as well as some sixty conspicuous women."

My curiosity was more than a little stirred by Aceti's reference to sixty conspicuous women among this Who's Who in the Calabrian Hall of Fame. Since Aceti did not volunteer any further information about these outstanding women, I am free to picture these sixty exemplars of womankind as embodying the soul of Mother Teresa, the talent of Sofonisba Anguissola (the first recorded woman painter to achieve any kind of recognition) and the political acumen of Geraldine Ferraro (the first woman to run for Vice-President of the United States). Of course, it may be that what made these sixty women conspicuous was not their sterling characters, but their passionate natures and feminine pulchritude. If this is what gained them distinction, if not notoriety, my image of these women would have to alter. Here the ancient model would be the goddess Aphrodite and in modern dress, Anna Magnani, Gina Lolobrigida and Sophia Loren.

While Aceti identified what may have been a Golden Age in the history of Calabria, I would have preferred to have been born earlier, during the time of the Renaissance. In keeping with my fantasy of having descended from royal lineage, I can imagine some connection between the Medici family, the great patrons of the arts, and my real father, whose profession was that of a sculptor. I can envision generations and generations ago, my great-great-great grandfather being banished from Florence after being forced into a duel with a neer-do-well member of the illustrious Medici family. This black sheep in the Medici family had cast aspersions related to the virginal character of my great-great-great grandfather's beloved, and he suffered the consequences in a duel.

Excommunicated by the Prince, my ancestor, a man of sterling character, followed the advice of his good friend, Marsilio Ficino, a celebrated Renaissance man who had written a classic text on how to live and enjoy life to the fullest. Wise in the ways of the world, my great-great-great grandfather eloped with his beloved and headed south to Calabria. Centuries later, through near-incestuous relationships, my father and mother were born. In retrospect, my long-ago grandparents would have been better advised to have stayed up north; in the south, they were forced to a life of hardship.

Knowing that this fantasy of an illustrious ancestry was a flight of my imagination did not stop me from a further indulgence—free-associating to the Calabria coat of arms which I found in *The World Book of Calabrias.* This illustrious emblem is described as follows: "silver: a gold cross of Jerusalem; in a silver quarter; three black eaglets without feet or beaks."

Were I on the couch of some Italian psychoanalyst, I would free-associate to the family crest as follows: "I like the look of silver better than the look of gold; silver seems warmer to me than gold and, as planetary metal, silver is related to the moon. One of my sons, the 'Italian Son', who loves to eat and is a gourmet cook, once dubbed me 'The Silver Fox,' because of my silver hair and the 'supple' way I deal with people. The gold cross of Jerusalem suggests that some of my ancestors were damn fools and went on a wild goose chase during the Crusades in quest of the Holy Grail—the closest I've come to Jerusalem is eating an artichoke—the silver quarter encasing three black eaglets, without feet or beaks, suggests castration, a feeling I had as a young boy (an eaglet) when I felt that my younger brother was my mother's favorite. Three is my favorite number which, on a carnal, secular level, I associate with the male genitalia, and on a spiritual, sacred level, with the Holy Trinity: Father, Son and Holy Ghost."

My mother was born in 1898 and christened Rosina Scarcelli in the Greek Orthodox Church of Santa Sofia d'Epiro. Five-hundred years before my mother was born, Santa Sophia was populated by refuges from Greece and Albania who fled the Turks. The Albanian people are among the most ancient on the Balkan Peninsula. The emigrants from Albania brought with them the Greek Orthodox religion and, in addition, the Arberish language—a dialect which connects two central tribes of the primordial Albanians, the Gege of the north and the Toske of the south.

I grew up hearing my mother and her relatives speak Italian, as well as Arberish, a language that is incomprehensible to me to this day. I suspect that it is because of my mother's "Greek" connection that I feel at home whenever I am with people whose heritage is Greek. It is more than coincidence that when I dance the slo hasapico in a line dance with Greek men and woman, I can sense Zorba in my bones.

My mother, keen on learning the ways of her new land, spoke only English to her children, although she spoke Italian to her father, who lived with us. In retrospect, I wish I had been forced to speak Italian to my parents.

There are few languages as beautiful to the ear as Italian, a favored language of grand opera. While I understand a good deal of the Italian language when it is spoken well, my ability to speak is limited to guidebook phrases. I did obtain a taste of formal Italian when I took a term of Italian in college. Reading Manzoni's master work, *I Promesi Spossi*, with its powerful description of the "Black Death" during the Middle Ages, made me appreciate the poetic flavor of the Italian language.

My father was born in 1894 and christened Ernesto Calabria in a Roman Catholic Church. I know next-to-nothing about my father's side of the family, other than they were diligent, hard-working people. I have only one photo of my paternal grandparents. My grandfather is wearing a dark suit with a vest, a white shirt with a tall collar, and a tie. Slim in build, he must have been strong, for his occupation was that of a mason. What is most striking about my grandfather in this photograph is his full white mustache which extends well beyond the sides of his face and matches in color the sparse white hair on his temples. His mustache, small face and twinkle in his eyes leaves me with the impression that he was a kind man, a gentle man, and someone I wish I had known.

My paternal grandmother's face is angular; her build, slim but sturdy. The steady expression in her eyes and her compressed lips announce a quiet determination. Seated, my grandfather standing erect beside her, her demeanor reminds me of that possessed by the pioneer women who drove across America to brave the hardships of the frontier. My grandmother bore five children, three boys and two girls, all of whom survived into adulthood. This was no mean feat when the countryside was periodically ravaged by epidemics of typhoid fever and cholera.

While information about my father's side of the family is sparse, I can relate a good deal more about my mother and her family. Unlike my father, who was an introvert and not given to talk much, my mother loved to talk, especially about herself. In addition, she was outspoken about everyone and everything in the world. When she became animated and took on the willful posture later associated with the Italian dictator, Mussolini, you knew just where you stood with her.

As a youngster, I did not press my parents about where they came from or what their lives were like before they came to America. As an adult, I wanted to find out about my roots. On our visits to see my mother and father with my family, I took these occasions to ask my mother about her early life. Without coaxing, she related stories of growing up in a small town, stories of her father and mother. She began with the story of how her parents met.

On the occasion of his visit to his aunt in Santa Sophia, my grandfather, while scouting around town, chanced to see my grandmother sunning herself outside the door of her home and thought she was the most beautiful girl he had ever seen. When he asked his aunt who this village beauty was, she congratulated him for "having a good eye." His aunt then revealed that she wanted him to meet this very girl who had just turned eighteen. Not long afterwards, being a man who knew what he wanted, my grandfather asked my grandmother for her hand in marriage.

Not everyone was happy with this match. My great grandmother was skeptical about my grandmother marrying a man more interested in "la dolce vita," the sweet life, than in "la buona vita," the good life. My great-grandmother was correct in regarding my grandfather as a pleasure-seeker who looked out for his own wellbeing first and last. Her warning, however, went unheeded, for my grandfather had already cast his spell.

My grandfather, in his youth, cut a dashing figure. He was robust in build, had a ruddy complexion, blue eyes and a prominent handle-bar mustache. When he began courting my grandmother, he presented himself carrying a cane and wearing a black cape with a red lining, high polished boots, and a feather in his large hat. The Sheik of Fuscaldo! Returning from a hunt, he would appear at my grandmother's house in full hunting attire with a shotgun slung over his shoulder. On the surface, my grandfather could have doubled for the part of a hero in a Max Sennett silent film.

Before the wedding, my grandfather had made it clear that he did not want his bride to wear the colorful streamers in her hair which was part of an Albanese wedding custom. He felt that these decorations detracted from the bride's natural beauty and said, "Custom be damned!" or words to that effect. I was told that from that time onward, that custom changed. My grandfather was a persuasive man.

At the wedding celebration, my grandmother was required to dance the tarantella, a spirited folk dance, first with all the "compares," important friends on both sides of the family. The bride then danced with her husband. A maestro-di-ballo saw to it that the bride changed partners while two musicians supplied the music—one man played the mandolin, the other the guitar.

After their marriage, my grandfather moved into his wife's parents' home. Soon thereafter, my grandmother became sickly and suffered severe arthritis. Her illness, however, did not deter my grandfather from making insistent demands upon her in the bedroom. She gave birth to nine children, but only four survived. Being the oldest child, it became my mother's lot to take care of her siblings, since her mother was not equal to the task.

My mother's stories of growing up have the ring of true Gothic romance. To begin with, she related how she met my father as the result of a ruse. That tale begins with my mother feeling impatient, a trait that worked for and against her in her long life which spanned eight decades. At the age of thirteen, she completed elementary school. That was as far as she could go in the small town of Santa Sophia. Her parents could not afford to send her to San Demetrio, which boasted a university. My mother remembered those days with some bitterness: "I always wanted to improve myself. I wanted to be something, a nurse or a school teacher, but I had no chance…stupid paese."

On her own initiative, she wrote to her aunt, her father's sister, who was a school teacher in the nearby town of Fuscaldo. Her aunt wrote her back and invited her to visit with the promise that she would help her continue her studies. With high hopes, my mother packed her books and took off for Fuscaldo. What she did not know, and it would take her some time to discover, was that her aunt had an ulterior motive in inviting her. My mother wanted to continue her studies and learn a profession; her aunt, who had no children of her own, wanted a bride for one of her two nephews.

Eager to get started with her education, my mother wondered why her aunt was full of excuses when she made inquiries about beginning school. After several weeks of procrastination, it became clear to my mother what her aunt had in mind. At age fourteen, my mother, more interested in school than boys, would have none of her aunt's schemes. Her dream of bettering herself would have been shattered had it not been for a fortuitous meeting with two sisters from a well-to-do family. They immediately liked my mother and befriended her.

My mother made the most of her frequent visits to the affluent home of her new-found friends and learned many things. She paid close attention to the domestics as they prepared exotic Italian dishes for the family. By observing the skills of the servants, she improved her own skills in tailoring, knitting, embroidering, and crocheting. After several months, when she returned to her home town, she put her newly acquired skills to good use. By the time my mother came to America, she had honed these skills so that there were few of my aunts who could justifiably claim to be in her league as a cook and homemaker.

Another event had momentous importance for my mother on this extended visit to her aunt. She met the man who would later become her husband. This meeting came about when my father learned that a cousin he had never met was visiting his aunt. Out of curiosity, he paid his aunt a visit and was smitten when he saw my mother. Though only fourteen years old, my mother's figure was well-developed; her appearance was more woman than girl. Additionally, what caught my father's eye was my mother's abundant chestnut-colored hair. My mother, in turn, was attracted to my father when she first saw him during a Sunday afternoon stroll in the piazza. Her impression of my father when they first met was favorable. She described him as "delicate, petite…a sheik." She added, "I wish this guy would be my boyfriend."

The timing for a budding romance between my mother and father was not propitious. My father had recently made plans to emigrate to America in search of opportunity not available to him at home. While he did not abandon his plan to leave Italy, he did alter it. The altered plan included saving part of his earnings so that, one day, he could send for my mother. Nine years would pass before my father's plan would become a reality.

One week after my father left, my mother's older brother, Frank, also booked passage to America. He had gotten word that his sister was attracting the attention of men in the town where she was staying. Frank quickly alerted my grandfather, who then wrote to my mother instructing her to return to Santa Sophia where she was needed. My mother knew that her mother, ailing with arthritis, did need her help. Homesick and always obedient to her father's wishes, she returned home.

In the years that followed, men continued to pursue her. "Yes," my mother said self-consciously, "I had a lot of boyfriends who wanted to marry me." One suitor hired a group of musicians to serenade her under the balcony of her bedroom window. During World War I, this suitor shot a soldier for maligning my mother's name. Her ardent admirer was sent to America by his family so that he might escape punishment.

But in America, this suitor's heart was still in Santa Sophia. He did eventually return to join the Italian army during W.W.I. Perhaps to cool his ardor while courting my mother, he consorted with a village prostitute, a practice not unusual among Mediterranean men. Intimacy with my mother was out of the question. When my mother learned of her suitor's behavior, she immediately severed the relationship. "The skunk ran away with her," she later told a friend. After this experience, my mother vowed that she would never date anyone who came from her town and she never did.

That my mother had a number of suitors is an impressive achievement when one takes into account that half the male population in her town had left for better prospects overseas. Those who remained were conscripted in the army and those who did return from the army were disabled in one way or another.

My mother's tales of being pursued in her young womanhood makes me wonder what my life would have been like if she had married one of her other suitors in Italy. My karma would certainly have been different. Coming to maturity in the thirties, I might have served in the Italian army. During Mussolini's campaign to regain the fame of the Roman Legions, I might have been a tank commander shooting at Ethiopians charging at me on their camels. Of course, I might have had other options, such as becoming a teacher or a member of the nearby Sicilian mafia. Had I become a college professor in Italy, as I was later to do in America, I would have had to trade prestige for making a decent living. Had I joined the mafia, I don't think I would have made it to the top to become a ruthless godfather who made people offers they could not refuse.

Despite the temptations she faced while being courted, my mother said she was clear about one thing: the necessity of remaining a virgin before she married. Throughout her soap-opera affairs, she assured me that she was always "a good girl." She did tell me the tale of one of her relatives who eloped and, after marriage, found that her husband was sterile. When the village mailman began making repeated calls to the newlyweds, it started tongues wagging but not for long. The couple eventually obtained three special deliveries from the mailman, packaged as two boys and a girl. I still can't figure out how this liaison was handled in a small town where gossip is a part of everyday conversation. I can only think that given the fact that Italians highly value children, the neighbors reasoned pragmatically that, in matters of family, the goal justified the means.

There are stories about my mother's earlier years which reveal one of her character traits, her tenacity. Still a child, my mother fell ill with typhoid fever. The epidemic had already resulted in a number of deaths in her village. But, in my mother's case, there was a miracle.

Perhaps, sensing that she might not live long—her father, a skilled carpenter and cabinet-maker had already begun making a small white coffin for his daughter—my mother availed herself of the privilege of the condemned person awaiting execution. She cried out for her favorite food: red hot peppers and eggs. Her wish granted, from that day forward, my mother began to recover.

Whether ingesting the red hot peppers worked in some homeopathic way by fighting fire with fire, or, whether there was a sympathetic connection between the hot peppers and my mother's emotional temperament, no one knows.

Of course, it may not have been the hot peppers and eggs at all which accounted for her miraculous recovery. A true believer in her early years, my mother may have prayed to the Virgin Mary for help and her call was answered. As a young child, she also survived a fall from the second-story balcony of her house.

My mother was also enterprising. She established herself as the seamstress in her town. Besides a thriving trade in tailoring, my mother wrote letters for parents who wanted to communicate with their sons in America or in the Italian army. This job she did not relish. For all these services, she received payment both in coin and farm produce. Her family in Italy never wanted for food during the difficult years of World War I, nor did her family in America want for food during the dark days of the Great Depression.

With the men in town away to America or war, my grandfather taught his daughter and a farm boy how to strum chords on the guitar. The trio played whenever the townspeople congregated for a celebration.

Never reluctant to work with her hands, my mother was called upon, on one occasion, to make a coffin. With her father away and some urgency to get the body underground, she agreed to tackle the job as long as it was understood that the coffin would not be fancy, with red-velvet inner lining or gold trim. But the box would be sufficiently serviceable, and would last until the soul of the deceased found a place to go, be it Heaven, Hell or Purgatory.

During one of her seasonal visits to Fuscaldo, my mother, now in her early twenties, received two marriage proposals during the same weekend. One proposal came from a college professor. The second suitor, besides being handsome, came from a cultured family. Following custom, her second suitor had his mother come down from Naples to see if her son had made a judicious choice. After a short meeting, mother and son were in agreement—she would make a suitable wife

Before my mother could accept this proposal, she needed to get her father's approval. Her father asked her if she loved her suitor and when she said she did, he gave her his consent, but with one proviso. Before she could finally act on the matter, she had to get her older brother Frank's approval, who was in America. As far as I could determine, no one bothered to ask my mother's mother how she felt about the matter.

It was three months before my mother received a reply from her brother. Along with his letter, two more arrived, one from my father and another from my mother's aunt. All three letters had the same urgent message: "Don't even think about a marriage in Italy; come to America to get married." My mother's reaction was: "Whatever my father and my brother say, I'll do." Later, she would say to me, "I'm here (in America) because I listened to my father and brother."

Having had that decision made for her, she had to break the news to her suitor from Naples, who had plied her with gifts of all kinds. Everyone in both families had a good cry when she broke the news. When my mother embarked from a port in Naples to America, her suitor's family continued to treat her as one of the family.

When the decision to come to America was made, her father said: "Either I go with you or you don't go!" That my grandfather would be abandoning his ailing wife in going to America was not as important to him as protecting the honor of his daughter. The fact that my mother was a grown woman who could handle herself seemed to matter little to my grandfather.

It was not unusual for fathers to be possessive of their daughters, but my grandfather's possessiveness bordered on the absurd. In Italy, he would never let my mother go to church alone. In America, his surveillance of my mother went to extremes.

The money my father sent to cover my mother's second-class passage was used for two tickets. This meant traveling steerage. In *The Italian American Family Album*, authors Dorothy and Thomas Hobbler refer to the journey across the Atlantic as the via dolorosa, the "sorrowful way." "Crammed into overcrowded berths stacked to the ceiling below decks, the immigrants breathed foul air, suffered from seasickness, contracted diseases, and continually feared that the ship would sink."

My mother's voyage to America began without hardships. During the first four days, the weather was mild. My grandfather played the violin and my mother the guitar; their music was welcomed by the passengers huddled together in every conceivable inch of space on the ship's deck. Then, the weather turned bad and passengers were flung back and forth across the deck of the ship, and my mother became severely seasick. For seventeen out of the twenty-one days of the trip, my mother was in the ship's hospital. She quickly recovered when they arrived at Ellis Island.

Ironically, had it not been for my grandfather accompanying my mother, her trip to America might have been delayed indefinitely. The year was 1921. Congress had passed severe restrictive laws limiting the number of immigrants from Italy and other southern European countries; few restrictions were placed on those immigrating from northern Europe and England. When my grandfather arrived with his daughter in Cosenza to make out an application for passage, they waited and waited for a reply. As luck would have it, when my grandfather made inquiries, he found that the clerk handling the applications was a boyhood friend from a town near his home. Their applications which lay at the bottom of a tall pile were shifted to the top.

That first step taken, there was still the obstacle of booking passage. Again, there was waiting and more waiting when they arrived in Naples. Once more, my grandfather was lucky. To pass time one afternoon, he went to a local movie. As he approached the ticket window, he heard two men debating who would treat the other to the movie. My grandfather heard them speaking Albanese. He interrupted their debate, addressed them in their dialect, and offered to buy tickets for both of them. When they inquired what my grandfather was doing so far from home, he vented his frustration about booking passage to America. The two men smiled at each other and informed him that they were emigration agents; their job was to book passage for those going to America. On the spot, they asked him how soon he wanted to leave. Within the week, father and daughter were on their way.

The voyage lasted from December 21, 1921, to January 10, 1922. The ordeal of the passage to America did not end when the pair reached Ellis Island. Upon their arrival, they were detained for four more days while my grandfather, just over the age of fifty, had to pass a stringent physical examination. Were he to fail it, both father and daughter would be sent back to Italy. Fortunately, my grandfather had the constitution of a bull and he passed.

My mother's journey to America began in uncertainty and ended in confusion. Because of schedule changes, when they finally arrived at the dock in New York Harbor, there was no one there to greet them. They managed to make themselves understood to the cab driver who took them to my aunt's house. He charged the two immigrants an exorbitant rate. Welcome to America!

CHAPTER TWO

▼

COMING TO AMERICA

There is no security in life, only opportunity.

Mark Twain

My father arrived in America in 1912. He was part of that mass migration of men, women and children who lived under deplorable conditions at home: overpopulation, economic collapse, crop failures and discrimination at the hands of the governmental power base in the north. The greatest number of immigrants came from the southern part of Italy where people were hard-pressed to make a decent living. What drew my father to America was the hope of improving his skill and furthering his prospects as an artist. In the nearby town of Catanzaro, he had pursued his studies with a talented sculptor, Alfredo

Alesandro. To go beyond this point in his training would have required moving to Florence, which his family could ill afford. In America, he would have an opportunity to advance himself.

It was my father's good fortune to arrive in America when there was a need for sculptors. Because of his talent and training as an artist, he was spared the drudgery of hard physical labor, the lot of most Italian immigrants who were unskilled. My father dreamed of becoming an architectural designer. He soon learned that his dream had to be abandoned for, even in America, not every dream came true. Disappointed, he followed the lead of other immigrant Italians who did what was possible with the resources at hand.

By day, my father worked as a sculptor; by night, he went to the Beaux Arts School where he studied with Colinski, a well known and respected sculptor. For nine years, he followed a strict regimen of work and study. All the while, he honored his promise to send money to his parents. At the same time, he began building a nest egg, for he had not forgotten the girl with the chestnut hair.

Coming to America, my father was fortunate in another regard. He had relatives ready to welcome him. He rented a room in the home of his Aunt Zia Francischina and Uncle Tom who owned a three-story house in East New York, in a residential section in Brooklyn. Aunt Zia remembers my father sitting at the dinner table appearing more boy than man, "quiet, a small figure lost in a big collar, his dark eyes prominent." It was in this house that my parents would live for three years after they married, and it was in this house that I was born. But I am well ahead of my story.

Zia Francischina established herself as the ruling matriarch among our relatives, the queen bee of the family. Like a Gibson Girl of the past century, she rode her bicycle to market, bustle and all. Her husband was something of a flirt with a wandering eye and a roving hand. To keep his eyes from wandering and his hands from roving, she made herself attractive when he returned home from work.

Ever since I can remember, Zia Francischina had a severe look. She had a high-pitched, scratchy voice and stringy white hair. Shrewd and parsimonious, this aunt sponsored a number of young members of the family who wanted to come to America; in exchange, she used their labor to keep her home spotless. Without children of her own, she housed her widowed half-sister and her three children, my Aunt Jenny, my Uncle Joe and my Aunt Mary. I remember visiting her home when I was a small boy and feeling awed by the high ceilings of the large living room, and the dining room with its mahogany furniture that glistened and smelled of furniture oil.

When they came to America, this aunt and uncle settled in Lancaster, Pennsylvania, in a neighborhood populated by German immigrants. Lancaster was a respectable place; the people were well dressed and well behaved. When the company my uncle worked for relocated to New York, the family moved to Sullivan Street in lower Manhattan. Unlike the quiet neighborhood from where they had come, Sullivan Street teemed with the noise of pushcarts and shouting vendors. During their brief stay in this tumultuous environment, my aunt and uncle, along with their four charges, lived in a tenement. They had to share one bathroom with a family that had seven children.

Within a year, the family moved to Saratoga Avenue in the Bedford Stuyvesant section of Brooklyn. For a short time, they lived in a cold-water flat; the toilet was a small closet in the back of the house. One night, Zia Francischina answered an urgent call of nature by going to the back house. She lifted her skirt in the dark and sat on the lap of an aged uncle who had established a prior claim. He was surprised; she was embarrassed.

As in Lancaster, their new neighborhood was predominantly German. With the encroachment of Italians to this location, the word was out: "Here come the Italians; there goes the neighborhood!" Sound familiar? In America, first the English claimed squatters rights; then came the French, the Spanish, the Scandinavians, the Germans, the

Irish, the Jews, the Italians, etc. The Statue of Liberty may have been a welcoming symbol to the masses who came streaming to American shores when my relatives arrived. But that message of the grand lady was lost on the street level. Each successive wave of immigrants became the object of prejudice by the groups who preceded them, newcomers who threatened their jobs. I wonder what would have happened to the Native American Indians, the only people who rightfully had a claim to America, had they not been hospitable to the Pilgrim. But look at what being hospitable cost the American Indian!

The German families in this new neighborhood where my aunt and uncle lived were surprised to see how clean and neatly dressed my Aunt Mary and Aunt Jenny and Uncle Joe were when they left for St. Benedict's Church on Sunday mornings. The nuns who taught at St. Benedict's School were German like their patron saint, but they were not overly saintly. My cousin Eugene remembers the time Sister Reginalda openly reprimanded an impoverished young Italian girl whose parents were unable to pay the monthly tuition. Her harsh pronouncement, "You Italians are all alike," was tempered when she noted my cousin sitting close by. The good sister added, "I don't mean you; you're the fine kind!"

During the decades of the tens and twenties, my father worked ornamenting the interiors of movie palaces like the Roxy and Paramount Theaters in New York City and the Fox Theater in Brooklyn. The Regina Pacis Church on 65th Street, in Brooklyn, is one of the few buildings still standing which show evidence of his skill. Long since gone are the models he made for the fabulous General Motors' "Futurama," at the New York World's Fair in 1939, when some 28,000 people lined up to see "The World of Tomorrow."

Among the statues he made that I particularly treasure are two small gems. One is a plaster model of a large peasant woman with a pudgy face, a true "Italian mamma," peeling potatoes; she has a contented look on her face which may indicate that she was thinking about her children while preparing the evening meal. The second statue is that of an old Italian fish peddler leaning back, looking up so that his calls of "catch of the day" will reach the upper floors of a tenement building. There is one detail in this sculpture that has an endearing touch—a cat is reaching up the sides of the pushcart.

After my father died, each of my four children, in turn, claimed one of his works to grace his or her home. As a sculptor, furnished with a photograph or model, my father did faithful reproductions of classic and modern designs. He drew his inspiration both from everyday life and from the realm of myth, from the world of the sacred and the secular. My father revered the works of Michelangelo. For one of his birthdays, I gave him an oversized book of the artist's works.

A note on obsolescence. When my father began his professional career in the United States in 1912, there were three hundred members of the Sculptor's Union. When my father died in his eighties, he may have been the last member of his guild. Today's buildings, for all their functional design, could do with a bit of the soul with which my father imbued his work.

My father took the subway from Brooklyn to Manhattan to arrive at his destination, a warehouse-size building, the Parsini Studios, where he worked alongside a dozen other sculptors. Each time he made this trip, he felt ill-at-ease. In the crowded trains during the rush hour, with passengers towering above him, he attempted to compensate for his short stature by adopting a samurai's defensive stance and placing his arms akimbo.

On January 10, 1921, my mother arrived in America. She was under constant surveillance by her father. "I couldn't go no place…the trouble he gave me." My cousin, Lydia, was enlisted as chaperon; she was nine years old. She would position herself between the couple but would be bumped to the outside after they had walked a block. My grandfather enforced the strict code of southern Italians regarding the courtship period: my mother and father were always to be in the presence of a chaperon; no kissing, or other form of intimacy, was allowed.

On June 17, 1921, my parents were married at City Hall. But this marriage did not satisfy my grandfather, who dismissed it as bogus, "…marriage Americana style." The following week, my parents returned to City Hall with my grandfather and a priest. They were married a second time. Even this arrangement did not satisfy my grandfather, who demanded that until they were married in a church, he did not consider them fully married. This injunction came from a man who never went to church and could not care less about being a Christian.

My mother remembers being anxious all during her courtship.On one occasion, when my mother and father had gone to see a movie, my grandfather claimed that they had gone to my father's studio before they returned home. In the presence of my father, he called my mother a "putana," a whore, and punched her in the face. Feeling distraught at having her eye blackened and face swollen, my mother became hysterical and began to pull out her hair. While her response might have given her emotional relief, it was a home remedy, a piece of steak applied to her eye, that reduced the swelling.

Nor was this the last unpleasant episode between father and daughter. When my father gave my mother a pocket book as a gift, my grandfather prohibited her from accepting it. These outbursts of jealousy reached a climax when my grandfather forbade my mother meeting my father's roommate. When she did, he left the house in a rage and vowed never to come to her wedding.

On October 1, 1921, my parents were married a third time in a church ceremony followed by a reception. My grandfather did not attend either church or reception despite repeated entreaties by many members of the family.

Two-hundred guests were present at the reception. The small band of musicians played mazurkas and waltzes and the traditional Italian dance, the lively tarantella. At the reception, the bride and groom handed a wrapped sandwich to each guest along with a small cupful of white sugar-coated almonds, an old world symbol of fertility. At the end of the evening, there was a grand march in which everyone participated. In coming to America, my mother had to abandon her trousseau. My father paid for everything.

Following the wedding, my parents lived in a cold-water flat for three months, until they moved to the house of her aunt and uncle. As was true of other ethnic groups who came to America, families clustered together. My Aunt Francischina and my Uncle Tom lived on the first floor of their home. My mother and father lived on the second floor. My Uncle Frank and Aunt Jenny lived on the third floor. The rest of the clan lived within easy walking distance.

Though my mother was a late arrival in America compared to many relatives who preceded her, and though she was regarded as the proverbial "greenhorn" when she first arrived, she soon established her presence in the family by quickly embracing the American values of individualism and independence. She proclaimed herself a modern woman who could stand on her own two feet.

Traditionally, males in southern Italian families are regarded as the heads of the families. Several of my uncles occupied that position, much to the pain of their spouses. From the start of the marriage, my mother was the decision maker. In my family, my mother was the center of the family, its leader and heartbeat. Her influence could be felt for what good and what bad happened in "la famiglia." While my father labored to gain security for our family, my mother sought to add status.

Within three years of their marriage, my parents had saved three thousand dollars for a down payment on a two-story brick building in a residential section of Bay Ridge, Brooklyn. My parents had realized the dream of many immigrants who came to America, the dream of owning their own house. They could take pride, not only in home ownership, but in having realized their dream without waiting a lifetime. They were the pioneers who first moved out from the Italian enclave that had formed in East New York. It would be another decade before the others would follow. Only after W.W.II, when my cousins began to marry, was there an exodus to Long Island and to the Midwest.

In taking this step forward, however, they never lost their "Italian soul" and the ways and customs of "la via vecchia." Through their patience, diligence, adaptability and resourcefulness, they declared themselves Americans, open to the ways and customs of "la via nuova." In taking this giant step, they changed their lives and mine forever.

Like many Italian immigrants who grew up with an authoritarian parent, my mother adjusted to her lot and had no long-lasting hard feelings toward her father. Following the old-world tradition of caring for parents, my mother invited her father to live with them, though my father was against the idea. My grandfather remained in my parents' home for thirty-three years, until he died in his mid eighties. Though he was the head of his family in Italy, it was my mother who took charge of her family in America, and, despite occasional flare-ups, my mother no longer yielded authority to her father or to anyone else.

My mother was generous, if not extravagant. She was outgoing, shrewd, tough and outspoken. Her favorite phrase in an argument was, "I say the truth." If there were differences of opinion with my father, my mother had a way to put him in his place with an imperious statement like, "You know nothing about it." Or, she might inquire of anyone witness to the exchange, "Am I right or wrong?" A complex person, her character was an amalgam of affection, pride, protectiveness, cunning, anger, vanity, boldness and intelligence. At her best and worst, she was a cross between Mother Teresa and Benito Mussolini.

The stereotypical image of the Italian mamma as scrupulous housekeeper, dynamic cook, prolific baby-maker and endless worrier who fussed over her children, goes a long way in describing my mother. Our home was always clean; a well-kept house was a symbol of a sound family. She went so far as to have plastic covering on our sofas. Plentiful food in our pantry was a sign of family affluence.

While my mother might attempt to occasionally impress others by the clothes she wore and how she dressed her children, there was little that was ostentatious in our home. Above all, my mother was careful that the opprobrium of creating "La Brutta Figura," coming off cheaply, could never be applied to her behavior.

My older cousins remember my mother fondly as a "party girl" who, at our house gatherings, persuaded everyone to perform should they have a special talent for singing, dancing, or playing an instrument. She kept an open house and was ready to "take out the store," to empty the contents of our refrigerator for any and all guests, at any time, day or night.

When my mother listened to the radio or watched television, her hands were never still. Skeins of wool were transformed into stockings and gloves to keep her children warm outdoors. Once the children were grown and out on their own, my mother crocheted one-hundred and twelve, eight-by-twelve-inch doilies. Each doily was monogrammed and sent to a family or friend. She also sent her monogrammed work to a "Who's Who" among celebrities she admired, particularly if they came from an Italian heritage. Frank Sinatra, Tony Bennett, Perry Como, Joe DiMaggio, Governor Cuomo, and the Pope received the fruits of her labor. She also sent doilies to other celebrities who were non-Italians but whom she favored: Lucille Ball, Harry Belafonte and Bob Hope, to name a few. Tony Bennett returned the favor by giving her one of his still-life paintings; Lucille Ball sent her a personal, hand-written note, thanking her.

In matters of motor skills, my mother was adept if not highly skilled; that is, in all skills save one. When my father attempted to teach her to drive our 1928 Studebaker, more often than not, she ended up driving up on someone's front lawn to stop the car. Each incident scared the hell out of my father who, though not a man to oppose his wife, finally took a strong stand on this matter. He forbade her from ever getting behind the wheel for fear that she would endanger the lives of his children, born and unborn.

Many of my earliest memories are associated with going to the beach at Coney Island with family and friends. The ride by automobile from home to beach took longer than it should have, for my father was an overly careful driver. When I heard the sound of rickety wooden boards as we crossed over a short bridge and smelled the fishy odor of the water of what we called "the perfume river," I knew we were nearing our destination. When my father was away at work, my mother took us to the beach on the subway train, a ride that lasted the better part of an hour.

Looking through our picture albums, I was surprised to discover how many shots were taken at Coney Island. In the earlier photos, all the women, my mother and aunts and friends of the family, wore unattractive, one-piece, dark bathing suits which covered up but did not disguise their ample figures. One of my aunts, who fit this description, always poked her fingers into my chest trying to tickle me, laughing all the while. She thought it was funny; I didn't. When I saw Neil Simon's play, The Sunshine Boys, where one comedian pokes his finger into the chest of his fellow vaudevillian, I clutched my chest as I remembered this aunt's insistent fingers.

Strangely, in several photos taken at the beach, both my father and grandfather are fully clothed, even wearing neckties. In one picture, I am standing, shivering in my bathing suit. When I look at this photo, I have the sense that as a small boy, I was not happy. I knew my mother favored my brother Ernie, four years younger than me, an attractive child who people fussed over. But, I also remember coming out of the cold ocean water and having my mother spoon out warm pastina from a mason jar and how good it tasted! That memory makes me want to believe that, perhaps, my childhood was not so unhappy. Could it be that both beliefs are true?

I was a late bloomer compared to my brother and sisters. I was slow to walk and to talk. From my mother's report, I was not an easy child to rear, especially during my first four years. She breast-fed me until I was eighteen months old, a longer time than she devoted to any of my siblings. She reported how she would walk me in a carriage for long periods of time hoping I would go to sleep, but the moment she stopped walking, I began crying. I resisted being held by anyone other than my mother. When she put me down in my crib I would begin to cry.

Even now, it embarrasses me to recall my mother telling me how angry she became when, soon after dressing me in a white suit, I would defecate in my pants. She spanked me and, to add insult to injury, she would publicly mimic my awkward walk after I had soiled myself.

As a parent, she had a low frustration level. Plagued by headaches since she was eighteen, my mother would wrap a dampened white cloth around her forehead. Her efforts to toilet train me took some three years. Had an Italian edition of Dr. Spock's manual on child rearing been available, it might have helped my mother as a parent, though I doubt she would have read it. She assumed that, as a self-respecting Italian mother, she automatically knew how best to raise a child.

It is no secret that there is often a close relationship between mother and son in Italian-American families. In the "hot-house" climate of "la familia," sons in particular can be "smother-loved." My brother, barely sixteen, eloped to escape her effusive demonstrations of affection. My mother had a powerful impact on all her children. Was there any connection between the way my mother related to both my sisters and the fact that they both married husbands who dominated them?

I know my relationship with my mother left an unhealthy imprint on my psyche. As a graduate student, I began to work through my difficulties with my mother by going to a psychotherapist for the better part of two years. When I turned fifty and began training to become a psychotherapist, those experiences with my mother had to be worked over again and again. Freud knew the power of the mother-child relationship during the early years.

On the positive side, when I was not yet in kindergarten, I remember the times my mother wrapped my socks around the bathroom hot-water pipe so that my feet would be warm after taking a bath. How good that felt. Nor can I ever forget those early birthdays when my mother layered a Drakes Sponge Cake with whipped cream and sliced Del Monte peaches. Not to forget her labors in cooking delicious meals, darning holes in my socks, and being there when I came home from school.

There can be no doubt—my mother ran the show both in and out of our home. At the point of leaving a party or a visit to one of our relatives, I can remember hearing the familiar refrain repeated by my father: "Andiamo Rosa." With coats and hats on, we waited and waited until she said her final goodbyes.

A strong woman physically, my mother was a "natural" boss. By temperament, she was given to playing roles one might see performed in the "commedia del'arte." On more than one occasion, I remember her response when I misbehaved. She would put her right hand sideways in her mouth and bite down on her index finger and knuckles. You could see her teeth had left marks. She would complete such gestures by waving her arm in the air as she invoked the Blessed Virgin to come to her aid, wailing, "Madonna Mia, Madonna Mia!"

Hardest for me to deal with was her way of instilling guilt. In addition to making me feel that I had inflicted the teeth marks on her finger, my mother would cry out, "What did I do to deserve this?" and "Haven't I suffered enough already?" Fortunately, having vented her emotion, she soon regained her equilibrium and life went on as usual. Whatever else might be said, life in my family was never dull.

Compared to Dr. Leo Buscaglia's child-rearing, my mother did not earn the high grades he gave his mother. "Dr. Love" remembers his mother as someone altogether wonderful. The way he describes his early upbringing, Mama Buscaglia did not stand for any nonsense from her son, Felice, as she alternately spooned out the polenta and potched him on the behind, apparently for undereating. Listening to the ebullient psychologist, I wonder if many people in the audience left his lectures with the whimsical notion that had they grown up in an Italian-American family, their lives might have been automatically happier. Let such Italiaphiles be forewarned.

Like my mother, several of my aunts would not have earned Dr. Buscaglia's unconditional praise. One aunt spoiled the romance of her son because his girlfriend had short thumbs. Another aunt undermined a fruitful relationship her son had developed with a woman who lived in a far-away state. As a consequence, he married a home-town girl who shut him out of their bedroom after the birth of their first and only child. Several of my cousins, practicing Catholics and thus influenced by the "Mother Church," remained in marriages that should have been dissolved years earlier.

A passionate woman in relating to her children, my mother was reserved in demonstrating any physical affection for my father. At home, it was my father who would make some gesture showing endearment toward my mother, a "carizza." Perhaps that is the way Italian women from the south were expected to behave toward their spouses. One sociologist I read commented that southern Italian women are educated for marriage only. Intimacy in marriage is not a high priority; mutual support and complementarity of roles between husband and wife is what is expected from both parties.

My father was away at work much of the time when I was growing up. Hence, I had less contact with him than with my mother. My father's whole life centered around two poles: his family and his work. He valued old-world virtues: hard work and the dignity of labor. His most important concern was providing for our well being. He neither drank, smoked, gambled nor became involved with women, vices practiced by several of my uncles who were the heads of their families. For the most part, my father was self-contained, a private man who kept his thoughts and feelings pretty much to himself.

I remember him as gentle in demeanor and easy going; he had a pleasant manner about him. There were a few occasions, however, when pushed by my mother to discipline the children, he gave me a few hard slaps on the behind. I felt worse for him than for myself when I saw that he had hurt his hand. Not a leader, my father tended to be self-effacing in interacting with others. Cautious with outsiders, his expressions of emotion were understated; perhaps this response was a form of self-protection.

My father's view of the world included responses which sociologist Salvatore Premeggia found characteristic of men from southern Italy: cynicism (my father, particularly in his later years, would say in a tone of semi-depression, "What's good about it?"); traditionalism (my father prized the old ways); marginality (he was never involved in politics or matters pertaining to the Catholic Church); personalism (he believed that an individual's word was his bond); familism (he felt that there was nothing more significant than attachment to the family); and work (he took pride in his work and the fact that his work provided for his family's welfare).

Serious in demeanor, there were not many times when I witnessed my father being playful. In one home video that was taken before I was born, I was surprised to see my father at a family gathering flitting carefree across the screen as he danced with my mother. Each time he passed in front of the camera, he had perched on his head one of a variety of outrageous hats or scarfs. Though it was not unusual to see him smile, with the passing years he became more quiet, which was due, in no small measure, to my mother's badgering.

My father loved his work. Never achievement-oriented, he measured his worth by the art he created with his hands. During the twenties, he had no problem fulfilling the role of the good provider. His skill as a sculptor was in great demand and he made a good deal of money. However, with the onset of the Great Depression, when survival was uppermost in many minds, there was little call for my father's skill. He became unemployed for some five years. Because we owned a house and had an automobile, he was unable to qualify for public assistance. My mother remembers him being depressed during those years to the point of tears. My father blamed himself, not the economic system, for his plight. With some bitterness, he would say, "You can't eat a house!"

My own memories of those dark times are mercifully vague. I do remember forcing myself to eat the dark, whole-wheat bread sent by the sisters of St. Patrick's Church. Before the Depression, I had only eaten the soft, white bread made by Silver Cup, the company that sponsored my favorite radio program, *The Lone Ranger.*

During those days which taxed the resources of many Americans, I do remember my mother doing piecework at home until the early morning hours, attaching bows and flowers to combs for pennies, or going to work at a nearby sweatshop putting lace on dresses. I also remember helping my father sandpaper four-inch-long plaster boats. He turned them out by the box, to be sold at Five-And-Ten Cents Stores. The most lasting effect of the depression upon me, until recent times, was being cautious about spending money. Even now, though I have the means, I still find it difficult to take a cab to a destination I might reach by strenuous walking. As I watch the cab meter run, it triggers my "depression mentality" and I think how much money I am needlessly spending.

My parents' home in Bay Ridge was the first stop that my father's relatives made when they emigrated to America. They moved on to Cincinnati to join other relatives. Years later, when they heard that I was going to be in Cincinnati to attend a convention, they invited me to round-the-clock lunches and dinners. Each meal was a bonanza, with a dozen or more relatives in attendance. At one meal, one of my cousins noticed that I was relishing the lentil soup they served and exclaimed in astonishment, "Francesco is eating the lentils!" He seemed to have the impression that anyone who had a doctorate degree would not eat what they considered common, everyday "peasant" food.

Remembering this episode in Cincinnati where I had shared my attention between profession and family, I recognize two allegiances which conflicted with one another: family vs. work. On the one hand, I had come to listen to papers read at the American Psychological Association Convention where my focus was to learn how members of my profession went about their business. On the other hand, my parents had urged me to visit my father's side of the family, relatives whom I hardly knew. What happened in this clash between profession and family was that, in this instance, the family won out.

At each bountiful meal, first at the home of one relative, then at another, I was served homemade wine. When I left the house to head for the convention hall, I was flying high. I don't remember anything that was said by the speakers at the symposiums, for when I made an attempt to write down notes, I found my pen trailing off the page.

Many years after this visit, my parents made a trip to Cincinnati. On that happy occasion, the Italian Sons of Italy Lodge gave my father a testimonial dinner in recognition of the hospitality he and my mother had shown the new arrivals to America.

In recent times, I have come in contact with organizations like the Federation of Italian-American Organizations which seeks to preserve the rich culture that Italians brought with them to America. Other ethnic groups are similarly motivated to pass on their heritage to their children, but it seems a losing battle. With each successive generation, the link to the past becomes weakened. Mark, whom I call our "Italian son," learned to cook from my mother and toured Italy on his own. Our younger daughter, Mayela, spent her college term abroad in Italy and can speak and gesture like an Italian.

During my early years, growing up a second-generation Italian-American, I felt embarrassed that my parents were not better educated. Had I been wiser I would have heeded the words of writer Agnes Medley: "But there were years when, in search of what I though was better, nobler things I denied these, my people and my family. I forgot the songs they sung—and most of their songs are now dead."

My parents did live to celebrate their 50th wedding anniversary. At this gala, my mother wore a small mink stole over her beige beaded dress. Relatives and friends came from far-away places. When the band played *The Anniversary Waltz*, my parents rose, and despite their considerable girth, they moved across the floor with more than a little grace. When I asked my mother to dance, I should not have been surprised when she lead me around the dance floor. Some things never change.

CHAPTER THREE

▼

MY FAMILY: WARTS AND ALL

Family: The we of me.

Carson McCullers

My mother, father, grandfather, two sisters and one brother made up my immediate family. My sister Jacqueline, two years older than me, was named after my mother's sister. My brother, Ernie, four years younger than me, was named after my father—well into adulthood the family called him Junior. My younger sister, Antoinette, born three years after my brother, was named after my mother's mother (I nick-named her Bieg). I was named after my paternal grandfather, who died before I was born.

My maternal grandfather, Tatamari, was a character, a genuine "piece of work." Despite the bad times he gave my parents before they were married, he agreed to come to live with them after the wedding. For some thirty years, I felt his daily presence, not only because he reeked of tobacco, but because of experiences which I shall soon relate. He lived well into his eighties and died with a full stomach.

My grandfather was lazy in all matters except those that pertained to his own amusements. I can't remember seeing him doing any work except for the times he would take his wheelbarrow around the neighborhood to collect junk to sell for pocket money. Perhaps his speciality as a carpenter, making wine barrels and coffins, convinced him that life was short–so why waste it on work?

On his afternoon searches, the closest thing he came to finding gold in the streets of America, that wishful fantasy of immigrants coming to the United States, was discovering dandelions growing out of cracks in the sidewalk and in vacant lots. My mother tossed the shoots of the "cicorias" into a salad or cooked them in a minestra.

In my mind's eye, I can see his rotund figure. My grandfather began his day with a cup of coffee and nothing more; then, out came his pipe. Next, he began reading the Italian daily, *Il Progresso*.

My grandfather ate only one real meal a day. At supper, he would reach into his vest pocket and draw out an all-purpose Swiss knife, open the largest blade and proceed to cut large slices of Italian bread. Whatever the meal, he would drink a large glass of the homemade wine he had helped my father make in our cellar. In a jocular mood, he would cut the peel from an orange all in one piece, shaping it into eyeglasses to place over his face. One of my grandfather's favorite imitations was of someone who, after hearing a joke, would open his mouth wide to emit laughter, but no sound would come forth and his face resumed a dead-pan expression like Buster Keaton in a silent movie. If I crunched down on an apple at the end of the meal, he would mimic the sound I made, a sound he wished he could make had he had sufficient teeth left in his mouth.

What I remember most vividly about my grandfather are the near disastrous encounters I had with him, especially in my early years. One day, when my brother and I were having a pillow fight in the living room, the pillow my brother aimed at me hit the newspaper my grandfather held before his face. The impact of the pillow jammed the pipe he was smoking into his mouth. As he slowly drew the stem of the pipe out of his mouth, he resembled Edgar Kennedy doing a "slow burn." Raising himself from the sofa, his wrath was something to behold. Not that my brother and I stood around to behold it. Had we done so, the living room would have become a "dying" room.

After he extracted the pipe from his mouth, his actions were enough to convince us never to have a pillow fight when he was in the room. My mother reported that in his rage, my grandfather went over to the dining room table, which was laden with heavy boxes. With one arm, he lifted a corner of the solid mahogany table high off the floor before letting it drop. This demonstration of strength would have made any weight-lifter envious. From the dining room, my grandfather chased my brother to the bathroom. I headed for the stairs and took headlong steps down and out the front door.

Fortunately for my brother, my grandfather was unable to gain entry to the bathroom. In his rage, he jiggled the door knob without success, despite the fact that the door was unlocked. When there was quiet outside and my brother prepared to quit the bathroom, he was horrified to discover that he had not locked the door. His feeling of security gave way to fear. He fantasized what would have happened to him had he been found out. Of course, my grandfather might have stopped just short of murdering his grandchild, since my brother was the proverbial apple of his eye. I shudder to think what would have happened to me had I not escaped. It was many hours later that I returned to the house with hope that his anger had cooled.

My grandfather, a skilled carpenter and cabinetmaker in Italy, abandoned his craft when he came to America. Though he had a workbench and tools in the cellar, I never saw him use them. Of course, the workbench and tools were off-limits to his grandchildren. One day, he caught me chopping a piece of wood with his ax. Not using common sense, or having the savvy of a boy scout, I made the cement floor my chopping block. The sound of the ax hitting the cement alerted my grandfather. As soon as I saw him, I fled. But I was not fast enough to make a clean escape. With ax in hand, he pursued me through the basement. When I was halfway up the stairs, he stuck one arm through the wooden railing and grabbed me by the left ankle. Had I not wiggled my leg free, my career in ballroom dancing would have never begun. Years after this episode, while watching the movie *Roots*, I winced when a slave owner cut the Achilles tendon of Kunta Kinte to cripple him after he tried to escape.

From the near tragic to the absurd! My grandfather was impressed by the Italian Pavilion constructed for the 1939 World's Fair. Inspired by this imaginatively designed building, my grandfather attempted to replicate this structure with a wooden model. The building at the World's Fair had atop its structure the goddess Roma. Below her was a long series of giant steps down which water cascaded. At the foot of the steps was an oversized figure of a female nude. The building was a monument to beauty. Not so my grandfather's replica. Though a perfectionist as a working carpenter in Italy, his model of the Italian Pavilion left much to be desired.

The disastrous flaw in his crude reconstruction had to do with the plumbing. At the informal unveiling of his creation in the basement, no sooner had he turned on the faucet, which fed water to his cascading steps, than all hell broke loose. Instead of the water flowing down the stairs, it came sputtering out of every opening in the floor model. Onlookers were showered with water. I could see that my grandfather's long, lazy sabbatical in America had caused his planning skills to atrophy. As a result of this fiasco, I decided to prepare my will, which stated that, in the eventuality of an untimely death, my grandfather was not to construct my coffin. I can imagine St. Peter examining my grandfather's shoddy work as I popped out of the box delivered to the pearly gates. I would not have gained admittance.

In addition to his vocation as a carpenter, my grandfather fancied himself a musician. Though he played the violin, mandolin and guitar, all poorly, he was not shy about performing or making others perform. When my godmother visited our family, my grandfather would immediately march her over to the piano even before she had a chance to remove her coat. He sat alongside her as she played Jaconda's *Dance of the Hours*. As a token of thanks, he allowed her to kiss his hand. With this behavior, my grandfather could have been a stand-in for the role of Don Corleone in film, *The Godfather*.

One dark, rainy night, my brother's boyhood friend, Tony Bennett, who later became a world-class singer of popular songs, rang our bell. There was no one at home that evening except my grandfather. The house was dark, with only one light shining at the top of the second-floor entrance. Bennett rang the bell and walked into the vestibule at the base of the stairs. After a time, on the landing above, my grandfather appeared bowing his violin; the sound of the instrument had an eerie quality. Bennett called up, "Is Ernie home?" In response, my grandfather peered down at the caller for a long, long while. Then, without any sign of acknowledgement, he slowly turned around and disappeared from the landing, bowing the violin as he went. My grandfather's ghostly performance left Bennett shaken as he left the house.

It might have been a scene out of a story written by Edgar Allan Poe. Nor was Tony Bennett the only one to have had this experience with my grandfather. At my brother's memorial service when Bennett related this story, several other musicians approached me later and told me that they had had the identical experience when they came to our house. To me, this episode only confirmed my suspicion that my grandfather was allied with the devil, someone who could curse his enemies with the "mal occhio," the "evil eye."

To the end of his days, my grandfather attempted to indulge his passions: wine, women and song. In the earlier years, when he helped my father make wine, he never drank to excess. Whatever his faults, I don't remember seeing him drunk. As to the matter of women, coming to America must have resulted in a good deal of sexual frustration, for he was lusty until the day he died. Whatever his life as a libertine in Italy, when he came to America, he had to sublimate his sexual drive by projecting himself into the fifty-two pornographic scenes pictured on a deck of playing cards I discovered on his bedroom dresser.

I never saw him consort with a woman, though I watched him making gestures, with sexual overtures, at our family gatherings. My grandfather had a ribald sense of humor. At family parties, he was not bashful in taking the limelight. When he sang *La Luna Mezzu O Mari* (the lyrics read "...the fisherman who would come and go, his fish always in his hand...,"), his gestures left little to the imagination. Whenever he had the opportunity, my grandfather would tell jokes with a bawdy flavor.

On Sunday mornings, my grandfather, then in his late seventies, would attempt to seduce full-bodied women on their way to St. Patrick's Church. Standing on the porch of our house, he promised, in his broken English, a pair of silk stockings to anyone who responded to his proposition. Of course, no one ever took him seriously but that didn't stop him from being on the porch the following Sunday. His figure round from eating and inactivity, when he rolled his eyes he looked like the figure of the sugar daddy who appeared in the cartoons of *Esquire.*

In matters of song, my grandfather was not the Caruso of the family. He wailed like a throaty-voiced gypsy when he sang an Italian love song. At parties, when he performed, he would become visibly riled if someone did not pay attention or show suitable appreciation for his singing. Recently, when I heard Luciano Pavarotti sing the lyrics to the Italian classic, *Caruso,* with the words, "Ti voglio bene, ti voglio bene assai" ("I love you, I love you very much"), I had a catch in my throat. I remembered my grandfather's lusty attempts at singing this song. At the core, my grandfather was a ham and, had circumstances been different, who knows, with his violin playing and clowning skills, he might have been the Jack Benny of the Italian vaudeville circuit.

Growing up a second-generation Italian-American, I heard several languages spoken around the house. My mother spoke to her children in English and to her father in Italian, for he understood little else. When relatives came to the states from her home town, my mother reverted to her native dialect Arberish.

In addition to English, Italian and Arberish, I heard a wreckage of the American language spoken by my grandfather, "Italglish." In this pseudo-language, English and Italian words were mangled together and came out as "ais bochs" for icebox, "ammoccia cheste" for how much is this, "baccausa" for back house, "broccolino" for Brooklyn, "ghella" for girl, "giobba" for job, "ma sciur" for certainly, "orriope" for hurry up, and "azzonoffo" for that's enough. If my grandfather liked you, he called you "sannemagogna" (son of a gun); if he didn't, he called you "sannemabicce" (son of a bitch).

Nor did these languages and pseudo tongues exhaust the way family members communicated. It is well documented that first- and second-generation Italian-Americans talk with their hands. There are open hand gestures when greeting others: "Hi" (Ciao!), "How're you doing?" (Come stai?) and "Goodbye!"(Arriverderci!). When my grandfather asked questions like: "What do you want?" (Che vuoi?); "What are you saying?"(Che dice?); or "What do I care?" (Che me ne fotto?), he would hunch up his shoulders, wrinkle his face, and place the extended finger of his right hand under his chin, pushing his lips together and narrowing his eyes.

Other common expressions and gestures he used were: "I forgot!" (Ho dimenticato!), accompanied by slapping the palm of his right hand against his forehead; "You're nuts!" (Hai pazzo!), pointing his finger to his brain as if he had a gun; and "You've got a thick head!" (Hai una testa dura!), placing his clenched fist on top of his head.

One observation about this use of body language is that a number of hand and face gestures center around the mouth area. Since Italians love to eat, this action should not be surprising. If my mother wanted me to know that I was a disgrace (disgraziato), she would bite the forefinger of her right hand. If my grandfather was angry and said "Damn you!" (Mannagia a te!), he would put the outstretched fingers of his right hand into his mouth sideways as if he were preparing to give me a back-handed karate chop. Or if he said, "Don't get me mad!" (Non farmi arrabiare!), he would clench the fingers of his right hand into a fist and put only his forefinger in his mouth.

My sister Jacqueline, though she was barely over five feet tall, was my "big sister." During my adolescent years, she taught me the social graces, how to be a gentleman. She gave me my first dance lesson. When I went into military service, it was she who sent me care packages, though my mother had a hand in supplying the contents of the packages. I never thanked her sufficiently for being my "big sister."

Having grown up under the domination of our mother, Jacqueline's marriage to a boy in the body of a man kept her in the position of being a slave to his wishes. A diligent and highly skilled secretary at work, my sister was prized by her employers. She had one daughter, Gina, who, unlike her mother, chose wisely in her marriage. My sister's relationship with her grandchildren was warm and affectionate. When her husband died as the result of an accident, Jacqueline became our mother's care-taker, a heavy cross to bear given our mother's daily recitative of infirmities. Not long after my sister retired, and shortly after our mother died, she had a fatal heart attack. At her funeral, one of our cousins may have hit close to the mark when he said, "It was as if Aunt Rosie called Jackie to be by her side."

I remember my younger sister Antoinette as a sweet child and a gentle woman. She worked in a bank and, like my older sister, married someone who was domineering. She had three children, two daughters and one son. Her younger daughter was stricken with encephalitis and died when still a young child. I have a vivid memory of crying as my brother and I dismantled Dawn's crib; it was one of the few times I allowed myself to experience the full impact of my grief. In her mid forties, my younger sister died. Through her protracted bout with cancer, her daughter and son remained at her side. I regret not having kept closer ties with both sisters, who deserved a better lot in life than they received.

I did keep close ties with my brother when we became adults. As children, I don't remember my brother as a playmate; as adolescents, because of our four-year age difference, we had separate friends. When we both married, we saw each other infrequently. In our later years, we formed a strong bond until the day he died.

Though it was never said out loud, Ernie was the favorite of both my mother and grandfather. My brother was the fair-haired child in more ways than one. The two of us were opposites, especially in our teen years. I was serious and studious, while he was playful and carefree. No doubt, it was his fun-loving personality which gained him favor with everyone he met. Ernie barely finished high school. Alongside the photo in his yearbook is his announced goal: Organized Crime. The only crime he could have been accused of committing during his adolescence was driving before he was of age. No doubt, during the early years, I was envious of the attention he received. It seemed unfair that I had to work hard for everything I obtained, while, for my brother, everything seemed to come easy. What I later realized is that his laid-back disposition worked both for and against him.

Ernie's abundant musical talent was a source of pride to the family. On one occasion, to encourage him to practice, my grandfather purchased a recording of a popular Italian folk melody, *Speranza Perduta*, played by a first-class mandolinist. With a grand gesture, my grandfather waved a five-dollar bill in the air and promised to give my six-year-old brother the money when he could reproduce the song on his mandolin.

My grandfather must have hoped that this challenge would engage my brother's attention for weeks, even months. Instead, an half-hour after my brother listened to the record in the bedroom, he played along with the recording, note for note, or so it seemed. I don't know whether my grandfather was elated or depressed by his grandson's performance. In all likelihood, he had mixed feelings; he was elated that he had judged my brother's natural talent accurately; he was depressed at losing the five dollars—a king's ransom.

Not a troublemaker exactly, Ernie was adventuresome as a young boy. He loved horses and could not resist being around them. One Sunday, after the polo matches at Fort Hamilton, a military installation across the street from our home, Ernie, ignoring regulations, followed one of the polo ponies back to its stable. For whatever reason, the horse became frightened, reared on its hind legs, spun around and landed one of its hooves on my brother's face and head. The non-commissioned officer who was leading the horse rushed my brother to a nearby hospital. After stitching the wounds, the surgeon told my parents that had the horseshoe penetrated one inch deeper, my brother would not have survived the accident.

Given my mother's emotional nature, the news of this near-fatality drove her, momentarily, out of her mind. Her shrieks and cries filled the air. With a touch of black humor, my brother related to me that the scar on his face gave him a certain notoriety when he entered high school. Knowing my brother, he probably told his friends that he had gotten marked in a gang rumble.

Just sixteen, Ernie married a schoolmate with whom he had become infatuated. When our mother learned of this, she became hysterical and tore out her hair. The marriage was soon annulled.

Ernie began his career as a professional musician in his late teens. During these early years, he played guitar with a jazz trio and, soon after, began his study of the classical guitar. My face beamed as I led the loud applause at the end of his concert before the prestigious New York

Classical Guitar Society. Ernie recorded a classical album of *Paganini's Sonatas for Violin and Guitar* (Boston Records).

My brother worked extensively as a studio musician. Ernie was Harry Belafonte's accompanist for nine years, with whom he recorded 14 albums. On one of their world tours, Ernie had an opportunity to play for Pablo Casals who commended him on his playing. Ernie remembered the great maestro speaking about "...doing something of overriding importance in your life." For Casals, playing the cello for a world audience was of overriding importance. Casals continued to play divine music into his nineties, even while suffering from rheumatoid arthritis. Ernie never forgot that meeting with one of the great men of our times.

Before he joined the Belafonte troupe, Ernie married a woman who had a young child. This second marriage, like the first, was ill-fated and after several years ended in divorce. Still later, Ernie married an attractive black woman who was talented both as a pianist and singer. They worked club dates together and wrote the music and lyrics to a dozen songs which were recorded on a long-playing record, *Barbara and Ernie—Prelude To*. This relationship lasted for more than twenty years before it ended in a divorce due to conflicts in temperaments and career plans.

Ernie worked extensively on cruise ships from 1979 to 1992 for Holland America, Sitmar and Cunard Lines, playing solo guitar and working with a ten-piece orchestra. Though he was four years younger, I always thought of Ernie as my older brother. Perhaps it was his lifestyle, being a musician and world traveler, that made me feel that he was my senior, even, in some ways, my mentor. Ernie drew his knowledge mainly from life experiences; he did not read many books. To my discomfort, he would sometimes introduce me to his friends, saying, "He's the intelligent one."

While attending college, I would visit my brother at his two-story, two-room apartment, located at the rear of a tenement building at 30th Street and 3rd Avenue, in Manhattan. I remember those early days when Ernie introduced me to the music of the legendary gypsy guitarist Django Reinhardt, and to the music of Ravel, Debussy and Shostakovich.

Later, after I married and moved to Schenectady, I often visited him while I was in New York training as a psychotherapist. Ernie always greeted me at the door with a smile and a hug. Out came the dried, hot sausage he had shopped for on Mulberry Street, to be savored with a bottle of homemade wine he had saved for my coming.

Ernie enjoyed traveling and wrote a number of perceptive descriptions of the people and the countries he visited. He had an equal appreciation for the world of art and, at one time, studied sculpture. He particularly prized his relationship with artists like Tony Bennett and famous portrait painter Everett Kinstler. In his later years, Ernie accompanied Bennett on a television special, *Runaway Life Styles with the Rich and Famous.*

During my visits, friends would drop over and it was party time. On one occasion, Tony Bennett called on his way to the Guggenheim Museum of Art—Bennett is a serious and talented painter. He invited Ernie and me to come along. As we drove in his white limousine, I felt like royalty. From the moment Bennett stepped out of the car, he was greeted by well-wishers. It took him a quarter of an hour to get from the street curb to the entrance of the museum.

After the museum, Bennett invited us to his favorite Italian restaurant where he was greeted with warmth but also deference. Bennett has always affirmed his Italian heritage; his father came from Calabria. We were barely seated when a man approached our table and thanked Tony for his music which he said had initiated the romance with his wife, who was seated at a nearby table.

From Ernie's small courtyard, in front of his cottage, you could look up at the Empire State Building and, on a clear night, see it lighted in all its glory. It was a magical sight. In later years, a high-rise building blocked this view and shut out the rays of the sun. Despite feeling he was boxed in, Ernie sought to beautify the entrance to his home with statuary he collected in his travels. During the week after Christmas,

Ernie went around the neighborhood and collected enough discarded trees to make a forest out of his little courtyard. On one occasion, I could hardly believe my ears when I heard him chastise a squirrel who had knocked over a flower pot. It was as if he were talking to a person with whom he had a bond, someone who had committed a thoughtless act and broken a trust, someone who needed to be confronted.

Ernie always remembered my birthdays and sent me greeting cards and letters from far-away places. In return, I wrote him long letters to keep him in touch with what was happening in the family. He had a natural way of relating to young and old alike. Whenever he visited me or any of our relatives, he would bring his guitar and play. In addition, a visit from Ernie meant fun for our children. With his bubble wand he created giant bubbles for the children to chase after and pop.

Two months after my seventieth birthday, a memorable event during which Ernie played the guitar as part of the evening's festivities, my brother had a fatal heart attack. He was sixty-six years old. His sudden death was a great shock to everyone. On his way to play a club date, amidst the traffic of New York City, he fell on the sidewalk and, despite the efforts of medics, never recovered.

The impact of his death struck me with full force when I went to the morgue to identify him. Mercifully, I had only to recognize him by a photo which, nonetheless, shocked me when I saw the contorted expression on his face. Two other strong images are connected with my brother's death. One is the bag containing his clothing. For a week, I could not bring myself to open this bag, after being told that when he had fallen, his clothes were slashed in the attempt to resuscitate him. The other image came from a dream I had when I stayed over at his apartment the night after he died. I dreamt that I went into a room that was frigid. I could see Ernie sitting motionless; his face had an icy blue tone like an iceberg.

At his memorial service in Saint Peter's Church in Manhattan, Reverend Lind, pastor to the jazz community, delivered the invocation.

I eulogized my brother for being the wonderful person he was and for being a great brother to me. Ernie willed me all his belongings. I treasure his guitar and continue to play it. In his last will and testament he wrote: "Any service performed should be in the nature of a celebration as I have viewed my life and experienced it as a gift. To all those I have known, loved and cherished, my very best wishes for their survival and fulfillment."

Following my eulogy, a number of Ernie's close friends paid their last tribute to him through words and music. Roy and Jackie Krall, my brother's "second family," before playing several duets, reminisced about their close relationship. Tony Bennett sang Kurt Weill's *Lost in the Stars,* a moving tribute to Ernie as his lifelong friend. Displayed on an easel in the chapel was a portrait of Ernie that Bennett had painted. The portrait is half in darkness and half in light. My brother was in contact with both worlds.

I held back my tears through the memorial service until Bucky Pizzarelli played a soulful rendition of *The Concerto De Aranjuez.* This music deeply affected me. I had lost my brother, who was dear to my heart, someone who had enriched my life beyond measure, someone who, by his death, had left a big gap in my life. I feel privileged to have been his brother. After the service, when we gathered for refreshments, Everett Kinstler offered his condolences. Among the many small treasures I found in going through the possessions Ernie left me was a book written by Kinstler with the inscription: "For Ernie, an artist and friend I admire."

Ernie loved and cherished beauty in all its forms. As much as formal art, my brother loved nature. In Manhattan, he would brave taxi cabs in order to ride his bicycle to Central Park and to Battery Park in lower Manhattan. Outside the city, in Big Indian in upstate New York, he found much pleasure in walking in the woods and being by a stream. In our telephone conversation two days before his death, Ernie told me that one of his dreams was to visit all of America's national parks. In his mailbox the day after his death was a video of America's national parks he had sent for, views of nature he would never see in his life.

Ernie had the makings of a Renaissance Man. His flaw in character was a lack of perseverance; he never fulfilled his abundant talent as a sculptor or musician. Ernie embraced life and attempted to live it to the fullest. He was beloved by his family and friends. In his last will and testament, Ernie wrote that he wished to be cremated and his ashes sprinkled in the ocean. I honored his wish by having two of his close friends sprinkle some of his ashes in the Caribbean, a location he frequented. But I buried the remainder under a lava rock in our Japanese garden. Everyday when I pass by, I bend down and touch this rock and greet my brother with "Hello, Ernie." This is a sacred ritual for me.

CHAPTER FOUR

▼

CATHOLICISM:
BEING A FACTORY SECOND

When God sneezed, I didn't know what to say.

Henny Youngman

The first time I learned that I had a soul was at St. Patrick's Elementary School. Our catechism was quite firm about the matter. Everyone has a soul given to us by God which makes us immortal and allows us to be united with him after we die, providing we behave. I don't think I understood what "soul" meant or, for that matter, "being immortal". What I did understand is that I could damn my soul to Hell by sinning. My first-grade teacher drilled us sufficiently from the catechism to firm up that connection. By the age of seven, I was schooled enough in examining my conscience to ask myself whether I had sinned and, if so, whether I was sorry.

I remember learning that there are two kinds of sins: mortal sins, that is, serious sinning like missing mass on Sunday, or cheating on a test; and venial sins, your common, everyday variety like lying, being disobedient, failing to say your prayers and fighting. In my early adolescence, I wrestled with the question of into which category of sins to put fantasizing impure thoughts and committing impure actions. The general rule seemed to be if what you are doing gives you pleasure, it is a sin. I learned that committing venial sins was not as bad as committing mortal sins, but if you accumulated enough of the everyday variety and didn't go to confession, you might very well end up, if not in Hell, then in Purgatory. You could spend a long time in Purgatory, say a million years, before you moved upstairs if, indeed, you were called at all.

The gist of the message imprinted in my brain from the beginning was that being a Catholic meant fighting a lifetime battle to avoid sinning and thence going to Hell. My image of God was that of a stern, vigilant judge. He was like The Shadow on the radio program I listened to–*The Shadow Knows!* What naturally reinforced this connection was learning that one of God's aliases was the Holy Ghost.

However grim your life could be with the Angel Gabriel's sword poised over your head, help was available in the form of your own Guardian Angel, assigned to you to help you make the right decision, especially when you were tempted by the Devil to sin. It was comforting to know that I could count on my Guardian Angel to watch over me forever.

Normally, if you were foolhardy enough to misbehave at St. Patrick's School back in the thirties, the accused, always found guilty, was sent down to the principal's office. More often than not, retribution came right on the spot. You stretched out the palm of your hand, or you bared your knuckles to receive a sufficient number of whacks from a ruler.

The message was clear and direct: Mend your ways! This treatment was given in full view of the class as a deterrent, a way of putting the fear of God in you and everyone else in the vicinity.

If your offense was deemed serious at St. Patrick's Elementary School, there were measures beyond the ruler and a visit to the principal's office. For serious offenders, there was the coal bin. Being sentenced to the coal bin was like being put in solitary confinement in a state prison. Of course, I didn't know what being in the coal bin was like until I was put there in second grade.

Being a well-behaved student, then and always, I don't know to this day what sin, venial or mortal, I had committed that put me in the coal bin. Had I offended the Father, the Son, the Holy Ghost, or even the Pope, and which judge had condemned me to this infernal place?

Whatever my offense, the punishment did not fit the crime. One fateful winter morning, I was marched out of the classroom by Sister Magellan, down the stairs to the school basement and locked in the coal bin.

The coal bin, so called, was a small, triangular, enclosed space under a stairwell in the basement of the school. At one time, it served as a place to store coal. Later, it was used to house errant students, a place where those who threatened the moral fabric of Christian society could reflect upon the errors of their ways.

After I had been incarcerated for what seemed a millennium, a classmate was sent to release me. Whether he could not find the coal bin or, out of sheer boyhood malice, my classmate left for lunch at home without releasing me. The location of the coal bin was a suitable place to instill terror in a child especially if the miscreant were put there just prior to the lunch break. When the school bell rang at noon time, I could hear the loud thump of footsteps as the departing students clunked down the stairs, eager to get home. Soon, there were no more footsteps, only dead quiet, except for my sobbing. I felt abandoned.

For all I knew, I was in Hell. True, there were no fires blazing, like in the pictures I'd seen, nor was there the Devil with his pitchfork grinning at souls frying in his torture chamber. I don't know how long I was in the coal bin, but it seemed an eternity. I remembered reading in my catechism that souls in Hell were damned to eternity.

When I did not return home promptly for lunch, my mother came searching for me. She eventually traced me to the coal bin. What bolted out of the dark enclosure was a frightened and half-crazed creature whose face was streaked with tears and coal dust. If you knew my mother, you would be right to guess that she raised one hell of a fracas. What else would an Italian mother, or any other mother, do when she found that her son had been badly treated? You can get an idea of how my mother reacted if you keep in mind that she could have been a stand-in for "Rosie The Riveter," the model for women during W.W.II. Let's not forget that my mother's first name was Rose.

Of course, there were apologies and some attempts at explanation from my second-grade teacher and the Mother Superior. Putting students who misbehaved in the coal bin was standard practice, my mother was told; all children who were unruly were sent there. It was unfortunate, my teacher explained, that the student who had been sent to release me had not followed the orders he had been given. Had I been susceptible to paranoia, I would have imagined that both my teacher and my schoolmate, the one who had been sent to release me, were secretly in alliance with the Devil. Had my superiors been consistent in their educational philosophy, my classmate should have been put on trial, found guilty, and following the practices of the Spanish Inquisition, put in the coal bin, a modern version of being stretched on the rack.

I might have felt some measure of consolation for the abuse had I been canonized a Christian martyr or, at a minimum, regarded as a child saint. But neither form of papal recognition was forthcoming. Barring this wish fulfillment, I might have felt mollified to learn that this method of chastising errant students was discontinued after my bout in Hell. I might have felt that, even at my early age, my life had had a purpose, that my life had served a noble cause. But this was not the case, for the very next week, another culprit suffered my fate. From a pedagogical point of view, I have to admit that this form of deterrent was effective, for I never made a return trip to the coal bin.

Although this episode infuriated my mother, she did not abandon the Roman Catholic Church. She had been raised in the tradition of the Greek Orthodox Church, which, in my mother's eyes, was sufficiently similar to the Roman Catholic Church. That she kept her affiliation to the religion of her youth was evident when, on several occasions, a man from her home town was welcomed at our home. Dressed like a priest, with a white collar, it puzzled me to learn that he was married. Whether my mother knew that the town of Santa Sophia had early ties to pagan customs, magical beliefs and even Muslim practices, I don't know. She did continue to send small contributions in support of St. Atanasio, the patron saint of Santa Sophia.

Coming to the states, my mother early on identified with the Roman Catholic Church probably because it stood for tradition, family and community. Despite the fact that our parish was dominated by Irish and German clergy, priests and sisters alike, my mother felt comforted that at least Monsignor Kelly, in charge of the parish, could speak her native language.

In light of the coal bin episode, it is needless to say that the nuns at St. Patrick's were disciplinarians par excellence. The Mother Superior, Sister Pulcaria, an Italian-American, was a disciplinarian of the first order. At the end of the semester, you had better have a good report card when she handed them out. On that Day of Judgment, a disapproving look from The Grand Inquisitor could unnerve the bravest soul, particularly a slothful student with borderline grades. From the moment the Mother Superior entered the classroom, her impressive girth, her malevolent facial expression, her black mustache, and the mole on her cheek which sprouted hair, kept everyone's attention riveted on her. Only after she left the room did I begin to breathe normally.

In the fourth grade, I was given recognition as the class artist. On Friday afternoons, a lay teacher was brought in to instruct our class in art; I was designated her assistant. What a sweet delight, what sensual pleasure it was to lean over the shoulder of the pretty girls in the class, and smell their clean hair as I guided their hands on the drawing paper. Importantly, this recognition as the class artist was the first intimation of what my vocation would be–a teacher.

My self-esteem took a giant upward swing when I won medals for two large pencil and crayon drawings entered in a city-wide art contest run by Wanamaker's Department Store in downtown Brooklyn. Of course, it helped to have a father who tutored me in creating my sketches, one a drawing of a castle, the other a pastoral scene. At the time, I had never seen an actual castle, though I could imagine what they were like from listening to my favorite radio program on Saturday mornings, *Let's Pretend*. Before the age of television and the advent of Disneyland, these half-hour broadcasts which dramatized wonderful fairy tales – *Sleeping Beauty, Rumplestiltskin* and *Jack in the Beanstalk* – fired my imagination.

In the classroom, we sat at individual desks. For the most part, the walls of the room were unadorned. There was no playground outside the school. If you arrived early, you milled around outside the doors and participated in horseplay. I don't remember ever going on field trips. I do remember taking part in a school play. I was the drummer boy who got shot during the Revolutionary War. What a sense of exhilaration I felt being on the stage, lying on my side, a bandage decorated with catsup around my head. Propped up on one arm, I clutched my heart. I was about to expire as a hero. Days after the performance, I went around school clutching at my chest, feeling brave; I had rallied to the call of my country. Little did I know that, many years later, I would be called up during W.W.II to reenact the same role; only, this time, it was for real.

Throughout my elementary school years, I was always a diligent student; in the lower grades, I was even a teacher's pet. At the end of the school day, I would be given the privilege of clapping the blackboard erasers on the outside landing that served as a fire exit. You could argue that my punishment in the second grade scared the hell out of me and influenced me to become a student who was serious about his studies. But neither the coal bin, nor having my knuckles rapped with a ruler or yardstick, was why I shaped up. I have always loved being a student, even to this day in my retirement. What the coal bin episode did teach me was that anyone in authority could do me harm if I was not careful. I never forgot that lesson.

St. Patrick's Church and St. Patrick's School were located a block from where I lived. These buildings were flanked by small houses and small stores. Across a large vacant lot behind the school was an old, dilapidated, abandoned house. To me, this house was haunted, and while I ventured around the exterior, I never was brave enough to go inside to see if it were really haunted. In front of the church, a trolley car rattled by. Both church and school have left indelible impressions upon me, some good and some bad. My overall feeling about growing up Catholic during those formative years is ambivalence.

For eight years, from ages six to fourteen, I was indoctrinated into two main rituals of the Catholic Church—I received my First Communion and made my Confirmation. In preparation for my First Communion, I memorized, by rote, the answers to questions like: "Who made the world?" and "Why did God make me?" Of course, our catechism supplied ready-made answers which I believed because I was told to believe. Only later was I able to recognize that my religious indoctrination followed the Ecclesiastical tradition, which stressed belief over a critical way of religion based on faith and reason.

On the day of my First Communion, I may have been fuzzy about the full meaning of this sacrament, but I looked good. My older cousin, a professional photographer whose first and last names were the same as

mine, photographed me in his studio. I wore a new navy blue suit—
short pants and a jacket—brown shoes, and brown stockings which
reached just below my knee. On my right arm, a white silk arm band
was prescribed for the occasion. Around my neck, I wore an over-sized,
white silk bow-tie, the kind I would later associate with decadent artists
who lived on the Left Bank in Paris. In addition, I wore white gloves; my
right arm hung straight down my side and in my left hand, which rested
upon an ornately carved bench, I held a prayer book. Rosary beads
encircled my fingers. A final touch of devoutness was evident in the
form of a white carnation I wore in the lapel of my jacket.

The symbolism in the Catholic ritual of First Communion is not
hard to fathom. The color white, the prayer book and rosary beads all
signify purity and reverence to God. In my picture, I embodied innocence and, had I been suddenly called from this earth by the Almighty, I
would have been appropriately dressed to enter the Kingdom of
Heaven. But after my First Communion, my state of grace didn't last
very long. Soon, I resumed my normal ways. As I changed into street
clothes, I went back to a daily round of venial sinning and occasionally
committing a mortal sin. Thank God for confession.

Reflecting upon this photo, I marvel at the mystery of childhood
innocence. I wonder how and why this pristine state is lost so quickly. In
my youth, I heard priests in Sunday sermons explain this loss of innocence by citing the story of Adam and Eve and what happened in the
Garden of Eden. The version I heard was that God forbade Adam and
Eve to eat the fruit of one particular tree. But Eve, being contrary, an
early feminist who stood up for her rights, went ahead and ate of the
Tree of Knowledge, and even seduced Adam into following suit. For
their disobedience, they were cast out of the Garden by God.

Did God not like his authority questioned or did the Almighty plan it
that way? Paul Tillich interprets this episode in the Garden as "the fortunate happy fall." If I understand him correctly, he means that it was a
fortunate, even "happy", fall because it meant the birth of conscience,

even consciousness, a peculiarly human achievement. With conscience, human beings were able to distinguish right from wrong.

Of course, there are other interpretations for the story of Adam and Eve and their expulsion. One explanation might be that on this fateful occasion, God came upon the naked couple frolicking under a tree, perhaps indulging in the pleasures of sex. Since this kind of activity distracted His tenants from keeping their minds on Him and spiritual concerns, He did not renew their lease and out they went. This explanation, however simplistic, does seem to be congruent with the practice of Catholic priests and nuns swearing an oath of celibacy.

Returning to the topic of childhood innocence, could it be that one way such innocence is lost is seeing our parents in the act of making love or even imagining them having intercourse? I never saw or heard my parents making love and my bedroom was right next to theirs. In fact, it is hard for me to imagine them making love, though I have proof positive that on at least four occasions they did come together. As far as losing my innocence, it was not due to sexual imagining; I lost my innocence after being sent to the coal bin.

By the time of my Confirmation, the Catholic ritual intended to change me from a boy into a man, I had long since become familiar with the many ways I could damn my soul. A master list of deadly sins had been compiled by the church fathers which I later learned found its way into Dante's *The Divine Comedy*. The list included: Gluttony, Lust, Avarice, Sloth, Pride, Envy and Anger. At the time of my confirmation, I would put Gluttony as the top temptation on this list. Being an Italian-American, it was difficult not to succumb to this sin of the flesh, especially because I eat with gusto. Fortunately, I weigh the same in my seventies as I did when I was seventeen. Of course, over the years my weight has fluctuated within ten pounds and my muscles have shifted around, and some muscles seem to have disappeared entirely.

Holy Communion and Confirmation are fraught with meaning, but the full impact of Catholic ritual did not strike me until I became an altar boy. I don't know what prompted me to become an altar boy. Perhaps, one of my teachers recommended me, or my mother urged me, or it seemed the natural thing to do as a Catholic boy. Whatever the reason, serving as an altar boy for a number of years did have a strong impact upon my psyche. I understand what anthropologists mean when they talk about the power of sacred ritual.

Serving High Mass, especially on Easter Sunday and Christmas Eve, was a liturgical feast for the senses: seeing the brilliantly adorned vestments of the priests in a setting of vaulted ceilings and varicolored stained-glass windows, hearing the swelling sounds from the church organ and the choir, smelling the pungent fragrance from the incense burner, moving around the altar, touching my knee to the ground in genuflection, and tasting the round wafer at Holy Communion. It was while serving as an altar boy at these High Masses that I had an intimation that the body and the spirit were somehow interconnected.

But what had an even greater impact on me than High Mass, which celebrated life, was the liturgy connected with the Mass for the Dead. I remember following Father Smith as he circled the casket, swinging the incense burner forward and back. The hypnotic motion of the incense burner, along with the smell of the incense which penetrated deeply into my nostrils, put me in a trance. Prayers were chanted for the dead as the organist played a dirge. What further heightened this experience was being positioned near the bereaved, seated in pews alongside the casket. The pained expressions on the tear-stained faces of family and friends made me feel uneasy. Participation in this sacred ritual was an awesome experience for a boy who had never known death in his family.

I remember, too, serving Low Mass at a cloistered convent located a mile from St. Patrick's Church. The service took place at six a.m., which meant getting up an hour earlier than usual. At the cloisters, I always sensed an air of mystery. I could hear the nuns chanting through a huge iron grate to the right of the altar, but I could not see any faces or bodies. It was all too ghostly. Following the mass, one nun took bodily form when we were given a glass of cold milk and coconut cookies. I still remember the twinkle in her eyes and can still taste those cookies.

There were four priests assigned to St. Patrick's Church during the thirties. Father Kelly was in charge and held the rank of Monsignor. He spoke fluent Italian, a talent which came in handy since a sizable number of the congregation were first- and second-generation Italian-Americans. Father Lynch was the jock among the priests and coached our baseball and football teams. Father Smith was young and handsome, a combination of Paul Newman and Robert Redford, someone to stir the fantasy of Catholic schoolgirls and, for that matter, the forbidden imaginings of their mothers. And then there was Farther Reardon, in charge of the altar boys. The Enforcer!

About Father Reardon I must confess having mixed feelings. During my five-year tenure as an altar boy, Father Reardon was the source of anguish but also, unwittingly, the instrument of much pleasure. About anguish and Father Reardon, despite having the best intentions, I don't think that I was adept at being an altar boy. Sometimes I would trip over my oversized cassock. When I lifted the heavy prayer missal set on one side of the altar, I uttered a quick prayer that I would succeed in carrying it to the other side of the altar without propelling myself headlong down the three short steps of the altar, over the altar railing, and into the lap of an Irish woman who was a pillar of the church.

A more serious concern was that I would forget to ring the bells at the appointed time in the mass, or would ring them prematurely. Another mistake was presenting the priest with a towel before I had poured the water on his hands. Most often, these blunders were overlooked by the other priests, but not by Father Reardon. At best, you could expect a lecture from the Enforcer; at worst, a not-so-playful knuckle-rap on the head.

Despite my ineptness, I won a measure of favor with each priest by attending to their idiosyncrasies. Monsignor Kelly, for example, lowered the chalice when I poured wine in preparation for serving Holy

Communion. His action, along with raising the cup when I poured in water, resulted in my pouring in more wine than usual. At the time, I did not know that mixing wine with water, "light wine," was a custom of the ancient Greeks and some modern Italians who do not want to get drunk. Secretly, I wondered whether Monsignor Kelly was a closet souse.

Serving mass, week after week, I began to feel more at ease and less anxious about making mistakes. However, it was because of my early experiences as an altar boy that I could empathize with what happened to a friend of mine. Joey was still a novice as an altar boy. Following Father Reardon to the altar rail, Joey held the small round tray below my chin to catch any fragments of the host that might fall to the ground. His hand shook uncontrollably with the result that he kept poking my Adam's apple. The effect this had on both the giver and receiver in this holiest of holy acts was something to behold. As Father Reardon took dead aim to deposit the host on my tongue, and with Joey poking the tray at my Adam's apple, my tongue kept flickering in and out of my mouth like a frog snapping flies out of the air. I never did find out what retribution followed after Joey served mass. Of one thing I am certain; my friend remembered that day for the rest of his life.

To be completely fair, Father Reardon was not all taskmaster. Once a year, he arranged an altar boy outing to Coney Island. We began our secular pilgrimage by having lunch at the Half-Moon Hotel which towered over the boardwalk. The menu was the same each year: Chicken ala King, which I regarded as haute cuisine. After lunch, Father Reardon took us to Steeplechase, the most exciting amusement park in Coney Island.

Ironically, if the intent of the altar boy outing to Coney Island was good, clean, Christian fun, in my case, the aim missed the mark. Serving mass at church and being foot-loose at Steeplechase were two very different experiences. In church, I prayed to the Virgin Mary to keep a tight rein on my impure thoughts. At Steeplechase, I freely indulged my erotic imagination. Though unsophisticated in the realm of logical discourse in my early teens, there did seem to be some incongruity in an altar boy going to Steeplechase. On that unholy day of the outing, I, an innocent, was being exposed to the pleasures of the flesh under the jurisdiction of the Holy Mother Church.

In church and school, I was warned against having impure thoughts and performing impure acts. I had been indoctrinated with the knowledge that I was born with Original Sin, like a factory second. Though I was told that this mark of Adam was exorcised by the ritual of baptism, I was cautioned that forever more I was to be vigilant against the forces of darkness which beckoned me to damnation and to Hell.

Lest you think I exaggerate the peril to body and soul in entering Steeplechase, here is a description of some of the severe tests that lay before me. At the main entrance to the amusement park, I had to traverse the Devil's Mouth, an amusement appropriately named. The idea was to keep upright as you made your way through a huge revolving barrel, a feat not easily managed with boys and girls flopping all over each other. Flopping meant falling over girls who lost their balance and revealed what was imagined but rarely seen. From my very first steps in Steeplechase, I could feel Satan's fiery breath down my neck.

After the Devil's Mouth there was the Cyclone, the scariest roller coaster ride ever. When the small car in which I sat reached the top of the tracks, I momentarily caught a glimpse of naked women down below in Ravenhall's Bath House adjoining the Cyclone. As the car started plunging down the steep decline, I felt little reassurance that I would survive this world since the safety bar I held, white-knuckled, felt loose, and rattled. I opened my mouth wide as we dove straight down the tracks and I attempted a quick Act of Contrition which, I hoped, might erase the sin I had committed in taking a quick peek at the women's naked bodies.

The next scariest ride in Steeplechase was the spinning tables. In order to get on them, you first had to go down a steep slide which propelled you on your back to a large platform with a dozen or so large discs revolving in opposite directions. Sliding off one disc, going clockwise, you spun onto another disc, going counterclockwise. Depending upon your position on the floor and the direction of the disc, you eventually got flung off to the side into a circular pit surrounding the spinning tables. Skinned knees and scraped elbows were par for the course. I wondered whether this amusement was meant as a punishment for not having voluntarily averted my gaze at those bodies in the Bath House.

What made Steeplechase famous were the mechanical horses which ran along rails, up and down small hills, veering sharply around corners. It was amazing to me that no one got hurt on this ride, since the safety measures were minimal. Here was a ride for couples on a date. Riding the horses gave you an excuse to hold your saddle partner close to your body as your hands encircled her waist. Needless to say, our altar boy outing did not include dates. But what happened after you exited from the Steeplechase Horses did have decided sexual overtones.

There was only one way to exit this ride. You had to walk across a spacious stage before a large audience of men, women and children. What made men howl, women guffaw, and children snicker was watching an unsuspecting woman trying to keep her dress from going skywards as she walked past small openings on the stage floor from which jets of air were released. After her initial surprise, each woman became wary and held her arms down by her side to keep her dress down where she was taught it ought to be. But just as she began to feel that she had control of the situation, a midget or a clown, circling the stage, would hit her on the behind with sticks which gave off small, electric sparks. This stimulus would completely unnerve an unsuspecting victim. Once again, up went her dress.

In later years, I had a sense of déjà vu' when I saw a publicity photo of Marilyn Monroe holding down her dress in *Some Like It Hot*. Unlike the unsuspecting women on the stage, Ms. Monroe had perfect control and knew exactly what was she was doing.

The question in everyone's mind or, at least, I blush to say, in my mind, was this: what was she wearing under her dress, if anything? This kind of questioning should not have been in the mind of an altar boy on an altar boy outing. Bill Feigenbaum, who worked the Steeplechase Horse Ride, reports in *It Happened in Brooklyn*, a delightful compendium of stories of people who had the good fortune, or misfortune, of growing up in Brooklyn, how surprised he was to discover that so many girls didn't wear panties. He remembers one woman, whom he estimated must have weighed 250 pounds, doing a belly dance on stage sans underpants. Though I would not have admitted it to anyone at the time, I secretly looked forward to the ride.

Could this Coney Island ride have been the forerunner of pornographic peep shows which were to become popular decades later? Or are we to see under-attiring the female body in a more positive light, a practice that has therapeutic value in freeing women of encumbering clothing like the corset of old? An orthodox psychoanalyst, of course, might have a field day interpreting this undergarment practice. He would probably attribute not wearing underpants to a woman's unconscious, exhibitionist sex wish. I will not comment further on this issue for fear of reprisals from my friends in the women's movement.

For altar boys who were wimps, Steeplechase also had rides like the bumper cars, which you could steer and bump into other cars and jar the hell out of everyone's neck, including your own. When several cars collided, the young man who worked this concession would jump from one car bumper to the next until he reached the heart of the jam and untangle it. I marveled at how nimble he was in his work. The Whip was another Steeplechase ride, but it was not one of my favorites. You sat with your partner in a car that swung along smoothly until you hit a corner, and suddenly, you were violently whipped around. At the time, I had not yet heard of chiropractors, although one would have come in handy after those rides.

I gained a new appreciation for the genius behind the idea of Steeplechase and Luna Park; the latter, before it burned down, had been the crowning glory of Coney Island amusement parks. John Barth's book, *Lost in the Funhouse*, puts the question: "For whom is the funhouse?" His reply: "Perhaps for lovers." Stripped to its basic essentials, Barth concludes that what Steeplechase provided was fun and sex. Under the guise of play, the idea was to bring guys and girls into close physical contact.

After the altar boy outing, I felt compelled on my next visit to the church confessional to slip in between my weekly recitative, talking back to my parents and teasing my older sister, my sins of shameful voyeurism and lascivious imaginings triggered by the outing. Strangely, my confession of sexual depravity did not bring a heavy penance from Father Reardon. I can only conjecture that since Father Reardon had arranged this outing which brought me to commit these sins, he was prone to reduce my penance. Or perhaps, I was too hard on myself in my youth and exaggerated the depths of depravity to which I had sunk. In any event, soon after leaving the confession box, I began fantasizing about next year's altar boy outing.

While on the subject of sex, there was this matter of masturbation which caused me to experience serious feelings of guilt and shame, especially during my early adolescent years. I remember reading a medical book at the neighborhood library in which masturbation was referred to as "self pollution." Well, I had heard the word "pollution" used in reference to Dyker Beach where I went swimming. Polluted meant not to swim there for fear of becoming infected. But "self pollution," that term had me puzzled. It was only years later that I realized "self pollution" was a euphemistic reference for "playing with yourself." Being an altar boy did not stop me from periodically indulging in this sin of the flesh.

After leaving the confessional, I was contrite and vowed never to pollute myself again. I was particularly careful to bless my forehead, lips and heart, making a tiny Sign of the Cross with my thumbnail. In my Act of Contrition, I beat my breast repeating to myself, *mea culpa, mea culpa, mea culpa.* With my head bowed and my hands folded in prayer, I vowed never again to commit such a black sin. Back home, of course, nature won out against culture as Freud predicted. I tried keeping myself pure but, alas, the next week I was back in the confessional.

I know that the Church Fathers wanted me to sublimate this drive and recommended taking cold showers. Gay Telese, in his book, *Unto The Son*, describes how Sister Rota soundly chastised him when she discovered him, one day, with one hand in his pocket as he sat at his desk. "Never," she instructed him and the rest of the class, "never put your hands in your pockets." She further cautioned students that when they went to sleep at night, they were to sleep on their backs. In this position, you were to place your arms across your chest with your hands on opposite shoulders. Assuming and maintaining this posture would make masturbation impossible. The only person I ever saw in that position was a corpse in an open casket.

My penance after I confessed this libidinous act, an act which I read could cause me to go blind, was six "Our Fathers" and six "Hail Marys." In later years, after I no longer went to confession, I wondered whether there is a codified list of penances for this sin of the flesh, or does your penance depend upon how the Father Confessor feels that day?

As an altar boy, it was unthinkable to imagine that priests indulged in this practice. Nor did my curiosity end there. Did nuns, under their starched habits, have breasts? And under their bonnets did they have short hair or were they completely bald? Answers to these questions pertaining to priests and nuns remained shrouded in mystery.

Though I never did satisfy my curiosity about such liturgical issues, I was shocked when my friend Joey told me stories of priests and nuns meeting in secret and breaking their vows of celibacy. It was like being told that there is no real Santa Claus. These stories left me more confused than ever, and while part of me was all ears, another part did not want to hear, much less believe, that any of what I was told was true.

Once a year, during the forty days preceding Easter, a learned Jesuit came to St. Patrick's to deliverer passionate sermons about the horrors inflicted upon Jesus—the scourging, the Crucifixion, the piercing of His side. It was during his sermons that I became acutely aware of the power of Catholic ritual: going through the Stations of the Cross; lighting holy candles; having ashes imprinted on my forehead; receiving dried palm leaves to shape into a cross to take home on Palm Sunday. I do remember making a special effort to be pure during this solemn, forty-day interval, and especially on Good Friday.

Years later, I took delight in reading Philip Roth's novel, *Portnoy's Complaint*. It would have been comforting to know during this period of adolescent turmoil that Jewish boys, like Christian boys, have this problem of self pollution. At the time, I didn't know that Christians and Jews had anything in common except their love of egg cream sodas.

The most approachable of our four parish priests was Father Lynch, whose brother Frank would later become my arch rival on the handball courts. Though I had failings as an altar boy, I was a good athlete and was selected to play on a number of sports teams. My favorite positions were catcher on the baseball team and tackle on the football team.

Though a good athlete, I was not a fighter. When the class bully, George Wagner, picked on me, I depended upon my friend Butch to come to my rescue. I remember having had only one real fight in my life. It was with Allie, a boy who lived around the block. We were about the same size and we punched each other senselessly all over the sidewalk. Strangely, I remember this fight as an exhilarating experience, bloody nose and all.

There was, however, one episode related to fist fighting that I'm glad Butch never found out about. In the early grades, I got into a fight with Mary McCarthy, who stood a head taller than me. I don't remember what started the fight. I do remember, however, that I did not fare too well. I attribute the victory of this young Amazon to two facts: her size and a lucky punch. My adversary's initial blow twisted my aviator cap around my head so that I could see only out of one eye. I must have looked like a Cyclops but felt more like a one-eyed midget. Half blinded and disoriented, my arms flailing wildly in the air, my adversary rained blows on my head with deadly accuracy.

This episode did undermine the macho image I was shaping for myself, an image based largely on movies about cowboys and swash-bucklers. In my boyhood naivete, I believed that any real boy was stronger than any girl, no matter how big she was. I have long since discarded this archaic notion, especially after seeing some of today's female body builders.

It may be that remembering this encounter is based on some deep-seated masochism which I sometime practice. What made this experience doubly humiliating, however, was not only being beaten by a girl, but being beaten while wearing my favorite aviator cap. Wearing it, with its long ear flaps and goggles, I often fantasized I was World War 1 flying ace Eddie Rickenbacker, ready to engage in a dog fight with Baron Von Richtoven. As an adult, I relish reading about Snoopy when he fantasizes flying his Sopwith Camel against The Red Baron in a dog fight. That cartoon, Snoopy in a dog fight, always gives me a chuckle.

Years after my encounter with Mary McCarthy, I was drawn to the Charles Atlas ad that appeared in magazines devoted to health. Charles Atlas's real name was Angelo Siciliano and he was born near the town of Acri, in Calabria, Italy. Numbering among his pupils Joe Di Maggio and Mahatma Gandhi, Atlas had one goal. These are his words: "All I want is to build a perfect race, a country of perfect human masterpieces." To this end, he advertised in the back covers of magazines that men would read. At the top, there was a large photo of Mr. Atlas flexing his tanned, muscular body. The caption below promised that any ninety-seven-pound weakling could be turned into a real man by using the Atlas System of Dynamic Tension.

The rest of the ad appeared in cartoon form. In the opening panel, the future hero lay on the beach, skinny and nondescript. A curvaceous female nearby pays him scant attention. Then the real drama begins. A hulk of a man, in the act of retrieving a beach ball, kicks sand in the face of the weakling. No apology is offered; in fact, there is no recognition that the weakling even exists. Understandably, the well-endowed female looks at the weakling with faint disgust.

If you don't know already, you can probably guess what happens next. The weakling reads the advertisement and the rest is soap opera history. Back to the beach and a repeat performance: hulk, beach ball, more sand in the face. But now the scenario changes. Brushing the sand from his face and body, the hero rouses himself, stands tall, flexes his latissimus dorsi muscles like an giant eagle spreading its wings, curls his biceps, and grunts. The hulk slouches away as our weakling-turned-hero is regarded with unabashed admiration by the goddess who becomes his companion for life.

Shortly after I turned sixteen, I did begin a regimen of body-building through lifting weights. Developing my physique had far-flung and important consequences which I could have hardly imagined at the time. It amazes me to think that so many salutary experiences happened by being humbled by Mary McCarthy. Had I known that this would happen, I might have thanked her instead of hating her.

My graduation picture from St. Patrick's School, dated February 1938, was taken in the school auditorium. I am seated in the first row of boys on the stage; the taller boys are in the row behind me. Below the stage stand the tall girls; in front of them, a row of girls is seated. There are twenty-five boys and eighteen girls. The girls appear much more mature than the boys. I never did date any of the girls in my graduation class.

A closer look at this picture reveals that no two girls are wearing the same dress or hat, while all the boys are dressed identically: navy blue suit, white shirt, dark tie and a carnation in the lapel. Each girl cradles a bouquet of flowers with one hand and her diploma with the other, while each boy clutches his diploma stiffly across his chest as if making the pledge of allegiance. At the center of the picture sits Father Reardon, flanked by girls. His expression is serious. I like to imagine that, at the moment the picture was taken, he was feeling some remorse for all the lumps he left on my head while functioning as my spiritual guide.

Since I never attended a St. Patrick's class reunion, when I periodically look at my graduation picture I cannot help but wonder what became of the boys and girls in my class. I am more than a little curious about John Henessey, the "brain" of the class; Butch Clifford, who always protected me from that class bully, George Wagner; Ruth Stevens, the girl with blonde hair that I worshipped from afar. What a surprise it would be to find out that the class nebbish, Julius Lamonica, had become a celebrity in show business, even though everyone was sure he was the least likely to succeed. A final thought—what memories, what expectations, did my classmates have about me?

My facial expression in my graduation picture is one of dead seriousness. Had I known what my future held in store for me, I might have softened my expression into that of a mysterious half-smile like Mona Lisa. My *School Day Memories Book* is another reminder of having spent eight significant years of my life with boys and girls whose names I can hardly remember. Some of those I do remember wrote the following in my graduation book: "Remember me as a link in the golden chain of friendship" (Joe Maresca, my best friend); "If writing in albums remembrance assures, With the greatest of pleasure, I'll write in yours" (Charles Murphy, the second smartest kid in class); "Remember Grant, Remember Lee, Forget them and remember me" (Leroy Brown, who was a head taller than me); "May your face never turn the color of this page" (Nettie, the girl next door, my first love); "God bless you and keep you always, Frank" (Sister Mancini, my graduating teacher); "If you see a monkey in a tree, Pull his tail and think of me" (Ernie, my brother); "May you ever on life's river, Have a safe and fairy boat, May you lightly, Oh so lightly, Over the peaceful waters float" (Lydia, my godmother).

After graduating from St. Patrick's Elementary School, I went to Boy's High School instead of St. Michael's. Both schools had excellent reputations. I don't know how it was that I chose Boy's High, a non-parochial school, instead of St. Michael's, which was closer to home. Most of my cousins had gone to Catholic high schools and, later, would go on to Catholic colleges. Perhaps, my choice was prompted by an inner sense that I had to break my umbilical cord to the Catholic Church.

Having made this choice, my allegiance to Catholicism weakened to the point where I attended mass infrequently and no longer went to confession. Of course, my mother was unhappy at my defection but did not press me to change my mind. Not so my godmother, who felt anguished at the direction I had taken, for she took her responsibility as my spiritual guide seriously. When she questioned me about the change, my reply, that I wanted to explore other world religions, was not well received. Her response was to the point. How could I hope to succeed in such an inquiry, a project that took scholars a lifetime to accomplish? What I did not say and could not say to her was that I felt smothered and confined by a religious doctrine that made me feel I was never good enough and always had to mind my ways for fear of damnation.

I am aware that in throwing out the bath water of Catholicism, muddied by its dogmatic stands on both spiritual and social issues, I had also thrown out the baby, a world religion embraced by millions of believers. Then and now, I have reservations over any belief system that suffers from the myopia reflected in the story reported in *It Happened In Brooklyn*. In a discussion about religion, Marnie Bernstein reminded her friend, Mary Quintero, a fervent Catholic, that Christ was a Jew. Mary's rejoinder: "He may have been once, but He isn't any more."

Unfortunately, because of this rift over religious beliefs, I became estranged from my godmother who, in my boyhood, was truly my fairy godmother, someone who always remembered my birthdays with a card and a gift. Fortunately, in my later years, we have reestablished the close relationship we once had. Because of our religious differences, however, we both lost precious years together. From this experience, I have a small appreciation of the cost, in human terms, of religious wars which plague western cultures to the present day.

I cherish many of the experiences I had growing up Catholic, particularly those connected with being an altar boy. Other indelible memories were left by the nuns who were my teachers. I remember their eyeglasses, their soapy scents, their smooth skin, their starched habits, their scrubbed faces, their flowing skirts, their shoes, their pitch pipes, their wraps, their soft hands, their deep pockets, their fountain pens, their names, their handwriting, the creases in their veils. There was something magical about their outward appearances, something I miss seeing in today's nuns dressed in modern garb.

It came as a surprise, decades after I had severed ties with the Catholic Church, that many of the scenarios in my night dreams reflected my early religious allegiance. The church fathers were wise; they knew that souls are formed and won during the early formative years when young minds and hearts are malleable. It does take the imaginative mind of the young to believe that there are millions of Catholics all sitting at the right hand of God.

CHAPTER FIVE

▼

FAMILY LOVES, FAMILY FEUDS

Fate chooses our relatives, we choose our friends.

Jacques Delille

Growing up a second-generation Italian-American meant being surrounded by "la famiglia." There were blood relatives, aunts and uncles, cousins, and godparents; not to forget the commares and compares who were intimate friends and venerated elders of the family. In addition, there were amici, those friends whose families commanded respect. In a strict, formal sense, all others who were not blood or family related were considered strangers or country cousins. This mosaic of family and friends left an indelible imprint on my character, stamping me an Italian-American.

My extended family came out of the woodwork whenever anyone was born, married or died. In one family wedding photo, all the relatives of the groom are grouped on one side of a gigantic horseshoe table, while the bride's relatives are on the other side. After the wedding, my parents rarely came in contact with the bride's side of the family. Still, weddings and funerals convinced me that I was not, and never would be, alone, an orphan.

When I was two years old, my mother and father moved away from the family enclave in East New York. Moving away did not mean that family ties had been weakened. Several weekends every month, my parents packed us into our 1928 Studebaker. The rule in our family was this: wherever my parents went, so did the children. The car ride to reach our destination took only a half-hour. One vivid and recurrent memory I have about our return trips was passing the large cemetery on Fort Hamilton Parkway. If I weren't asleep when we approached this location, a place which filled me with fright, I would duck down in the back seat of the car. I imagined that some ghost would reach through the window and drag me screaming out of the car into the cemetery and leave me on a tombstone while a chain of corpses did a macabre dance around me.

Among first-generation Italian-Americans, a special place is accorded to godparents. A photograph of my baptism shows me in my mother's arms. My cousin Lydia, my godmother, is only fourteen years old, though she looks mature well beyond her years. In the center of the baptismal photo, my godfather, my uncle Frank, is standing with my cousin Michael in his arms. Unlike the soft expression on my godmother's face, my godfather's look is stern. His forehead is topped by a full head of hair, one eye is slightly closed, the other opened wide. His face announces that he is determined to get his way.

My mother's choice of her older brother as my godfather was ill-advised. An altar boy in his youth, by the time he came to America he had long since broken his ties to the Catholic Church. Unlike my godmother, my godfather showed little interest in or affection for his godson. He was particularly hard on me for reasons known only to himself.

One Saturday afternoon, when I was eight years old, he and I were carrying sticks of firewood from the backyard of our home to the cellar. Our basement was poorly lighted and after going down a short flight of cement stairs, he tripped over a pipe which stood above the floor surface. Following close behind him, I also tripped over the pipe.

We made a second trip and this time, he stepped over the pipe and I tripped over it again. In a voice that carried more than a touch of sarcasm, he turned to me and said, "You see, compare, that is the difference between you and me. I am intelligent and you are stupid." This judgment coming from someone who towered above me, someone I was taught to respect, made me sufficiently anxious so that on entering the basement a third time, I tripped over the pipe again as he predicted I would. Each time I recall this episode, I am filled with anger.

In 1918, when he was twenty-two, Uncle Frank enlisted in the army and was assigned to play the clarinet in the 115th Infantry Band. He embarked on an Italian ocean liner to France and, because of his ability to speak Italian, he was commandeered to be an interpreter for the American officers abroad. He ate and drank with his military superiors and enjoyed the role that came easily to him, a carouser. I remember seeing a three-foot-tall photo of him in full combat uniform. He wore a steel helmet and had on all the gear of an infantry soldier ready for action. In this photo, he looked formidable enough to take on the whole German army. At one of the forward camps to which he was sent during the Argonne offensive in France, he remembered an artillery barrage which forced him to dive into a foxhole. Fortunately, the war ended when he had been in service for less than a year.

Looking at my uncle's discharge papers, signed by the commander in chief of the American Expeditionary Forces, General Pershing, what surprised me most was learning that he was listed as being five feet, six and a quarter inches tall. As a child, my uncle always appeared larger than life, someone who towered over me. Even as an adult, I thought he was taller than me (my discharge papers list me as five feet, seven inches.) What further surprised me was hearing that while in France, my uncle wrote ardent love letters to his wife.

After he returned home, his ardor turned to carousing with his drinking buddies, whom he would invite home at 3 a.m.. He would then summon his wife to get up and make pasta for them all. Before the family sat down to a meal, his son would have to go to the corner bar to urge him to come home so that the family could have supper. Despite these stories, I never remember seeing my godfather drunk.

Uncle Frank was a man of intelligence, a skilled carpenter but an unreliable contractor. I was amazed to see the meticulous blueprints he had drawn for one of the construction jobs in the Roman Ornamental Plastering Company he owned. While he took pride in doing a job right and would be unmerciful in criticizing his younger brother, my Uncle Pepino, for what he judged poor work, he did not always finish the jobs he started. I often heard him say, "I'm in the hands of the receivers," which meant he was always being pursued by bill collectors.

Despite residual resentments toward my godfather, I also have pleasant memories associated with him. He organized a quartet which consisted of my brother, me, and two of our cousins. My cousin Michael and I played guitars, while my cousin Eugene and my brother played mandolins. Periodically, Uncle Frank would join our group when we rehearsed in the small kitchen of his apartment flat, along with my Aunt Jenny who pounded out chords on the piano. The music he selected came from popular tunes of the day, *It's a Sin to Tell a Lie* and *Moon of Manacura*. In preparation for family parties, we practiced mazurkas and waltzes to dance to, folk melodies like *Guitarra Romana* and *Speranza Perduta*. Recently, I was invited to join a group of musicians whose goal it was to bring back the old Italians tunes I enjoyed playing. As I strummed along on my guitar playing the chords to *Speranza Perduta*, I was flooded with delicious memories of those years gone by.

Our music teacher, one of my uncle's drinking buddies, was a character out of a Damon Runyon story. Mr. Russo was a musician, but, like my uncle, he had difficulty concentrating on his role as teacher. One time, he arrived half drunk for the lesson; in a slumped-over position, he began writing on a page of music only to end up trailing his notations onto the table. During another lesson, he asked me to bring him ink. When I returned with the bottle of ink, with a sheepish grin he replied, "Not that kind; the red kind!" When his mind was clear, he could be wily like a fox. Knowing that my brother would rely on his ear to play an appointed piece of music, Mr. Russo would announce the name of one selection but place the music of another selection on the stand. When my brother proceeded to play the wrong selection, our teacher exclaimed in glee, "Aha!"

I have moments of sadness when I think of the progress I might have made playing the classical guitar had I studied with a more conscientious teacher, someone who was first-rate. Not that my parents would have thought it important or affordable to engage a first-rate teacher. Still, my fantasy is that I might have come a bit closer to playing like Segovia or Julian Bream had I had a more dedicated teacher.

Over the years to the present day, I have continued to take lessons on the classical guitar. My current instructor, Maria Zemantouski, is a gifted teacher and performer; she is outstanding as a flamenco guitarist. When we play duets and I have an opportunity to improvise with her on a bolero or blues, time stands still. There are no words for it.

Of all art forms, music gives me the most pleasure. Whenever I am at a concert and am able to sit close to the stage, my rapt attention on the performers does not go unnoticed. At the end of the program, when I approach these artists to thank them for their performance, often their response is as enthusiastic as mine; they attempt to outdo themselves. We have "played off one another." Soul to soul!

Back to my musical beginnings. Our quartet, in those early days, did gain a modicum of recognition beyond family praise. We entered an amateur contest at the Harbor Theater where I spent long Saturday afternoons seeing double features. The contest we entered was modeled on the then-popular radio show, *The Major Bowes Amateur Hour*. We were given second prize by the emcee, though the audience's applause indicated that we should have been awarded first prize.

On some weekends when we rehearsed with our quartet, I was allowed to sleep over at my godfather's house. His son, Michael, my first cousin, was a year older than me and streetwise. The Little Italy neighborhood around McDougall Street where he lived had an air of excitement missing in the more residential neighborhood where I lived. From the moment we stepped out of the door of his apartment, I felt a sense of excitement. On the street, there was always a stick ball game in progress. While the boys took their turns at bat, girls, in clusters of twos and threes, came by to flirt. One evening, my cousin took me to a house in the neighborhood and told me to look up at the second-floor window. I got a fleeting glimpse of a teenage girl disrobing; momentarily, her budding breasts were exposed.

I was in awe watching my older cousins play baseball in full uniform. They called themselves "The Romers." They expected their younger cousins to do their bidding and were not above playing tricks. My cousin, Alfred, told me to go down the street to catch a ball. Each time I paused awaiting his throw, he would signal me to go farther back. When I was practically out of sight, he laughed, turned around, and went into his house. I felt like a fool.

Occasionally, on a weekend sleep-over, our quartet would play at the Sumpter Street Men's Social Club. Following our performance, a black piano player who looked like Fats Waller, accompanied by a white drummer, played blues and popular standards. It was my earliest introduction to jazz and I never lost my taste for it. Competitive street games, flirting girls, peep show erotics and hot jazz were an aphrodisiac to an altar boy not yet fully weaned from the Mother Church.

Uncle Joe, the father of my godmother, impressed me as being a stand-up, no-nonsense type of man. Born in the United States, his family went back to Italy where he received his early schooling. My older cousins referred to him as "The Governor," probably because through his job selling insurance he became knowledgeable about money matters. Always pleasant to me, he called me "Fey."

When my parents were newly married, my uncle Joe, my uncle Frank, and my uncle Sal went to a masquerade ball as "The Three Musketeers." On that evening, they may have felt like Alexander Dumas' characters, "One for all and all for one!" For a number of years, our families were "one for all." We got together at parties in the basement of my uncle Joe's house where special foods were prepared and everyone danced.

Unhappily for all our families, that sentiment of solidarity did not last. When Uncle Frank did not keep up car payments on the automobile Uncle Joe helped him finance, Uncle Frank resented his repossessing the automobile and refusing to return it to him. That episode started a feud that was to last twenty-five years. No longer did everyone come to the same celebrations and families were forced to split their loyalties. With the passage of time, our families were reunited. Ironically, neither uncle knows that he is buried next to the other in the same family plot.

Not long after this foray into the world of show business, my brother and I entered a Bora Minevitch harmonica contest sponsored by the same theater. The Bora Minevitch Harmonica Ensemble appeared to be a ragtag band of harmonica players but, in fact, were first-rate musicians. In addition to performing on a range of harmonicas, the band members fooled around on stage. One player, a midget who played an oversized harmonica, would periodically bite or kick a fellow musician in the leg and scurry to the other side of the stage to seek the protection of the band leader. The harmonica contest we entered went on for four weeks. The first week, my brother won first prize; the second week, I won first prize. When it came time for the final playoffs, my brother's obvious ability along with his young age—he was six years old—easily made him the all-around winner.

Divisions in our family were not only created by my uncles who felt their sense of pride and honor had been hurt. My mother was not one to take lightly what she considered an insult or an offense. There was one volatile incident that took place when we visited "Ingenieri," so called after his profession. He had one glass eye and a balding head with several strands of hair crossing from one side to the other. My mother tried to match him with my cousin Lydia, who would have none of him. He married Congetta who considered herself in a class above my mother. On one visit to their home, my mother rang the bell but received no response. She circled the house and called down an open window in the basement. Suddenly, Congetta slammed the window in her face. Furious at this show of hostility, my mother put her fist through the window, which resulted in her having to have a number of stitches in her hand. While the wound in her hand eventually healed, her relationship with this couple never did.

Before the feuding began between my two uncles, our home was a frequent meeting place, particularly on Sunday afternoons; we would sit at the dinner table for hours at a time. During one Sunday dinner as we went from one special course to the next, one of my aunts, in the middle of the meal, audibly farted. Her facial expression suggested that she was in discomfort so we attributed this gastric outburst to a stomach upset. After her apology, we continued with the meal. But soon, there was another report, louder than the one before. Knowing her to be the clown aunt of the family, we all began to suspect that she was up to one of her tricks—and she was. At the second firing, my father could not stop himself from laughing and he joined in with a report of his own.

No longer able to keep a straight face, this aunt uncovered her flatulence machine and demonstrated how it worked. At that point, everyone, young and old, wanted to give the gadget a try. With each new demonstration, there were fresh gales of laughter to the point of tears. The decorum of the dinner table was shattered and, had there been any boundaries between social class, economic status, as well as age, they would have dissolved. I am certain that had Emily Post heard of this episode, our family might have been put in print as an example of uncivilized behavior. By the way, the Italian word for fart, "scorreggia," even sounds like what it stands for if you put the emphasis on the double R.

Now to some technical details about this ingenious contraption. The flatulence machine can be assembled by one without a degree in mechanical engineering. You take a wire coat hanger, bend it into a U shape, small enough to settle under one buttock. Between the two poles of the U shaped coat hanger, you attach a medium sized metal washer to the end of two thick rubber bands strung to either pole. A technical manual, should one exist, would instruct you to twist the washer counterclockwise before placing the primed mechanism under the buttock of your choice. By tilting one cheek to the side, you release the mechanism.

The manual should add that you allow a few minutes after the first release, to rewind the mechanism, unobserved, under the edge of the tablecloth. The interval during which you prepare for a second blast will give dinner guests time to muse about how little control we have over nature and our bodily functions.

Out of curiosity, I wondered if the subject of flatulence had received serious treatment in the scientific literature. I mused that many individuals would wish to be enlightened about how to enhance their ability to predict and control this form of interpersonal communication. I am happy to report that I did find one reference in the *Journal of Polymorphous Perversity* with the title "Cognitive-Behavioral Treatment of Chronic Flatulence." The article was the report of a ten-session training program run by an experienced flatulence therapist whom the subjects named "Windbreaker." Episodes when subjects flatulated were rated by three judges on the following dimensions: (1) duration; (2) loudness; (3) pitch; (4) tonal quality; (5) fragrance. Though the results of this investigation were inconclusive, one subject, known as "Boomer," reported: "I believe that this is a very important and long neglected area of research."

It was always a source of amazement to me that this aunt who reminded me of the cartoon character Betty Boop was married to a man who never smiled or laughed and was a bore to boot. Perhaps, having this lifetime partner, my aunt had to resort to humor to keep her sanity. She worked as a saleswoman in Namm's Department Store and must have been good at her work. I remember a story she told me which she probably fabricated. One day, an elderly woman fainted on the floor of the department store. As people crowded around the fallen body, someone shouted, "Get her some water." The woman raised her head and said in a Jewish accent, "Make it a malted."

Many years after the charade with her flatulence machine, I met this aunt at a funeral. I blurted out without thinking, "Are you still around?" Picking up on my cue, as if I were the straight-man in a comedy routine, she turned her head slowly, now looking over her right shoulder, then over her left, to verify that I was indeed addressing her and not someone else. Then she looked me straight in the eye and replied in a tone of feigned innocence, "Where else should I be?"

I don't know, to this day, what prompted my greeting her in this manner, but I do know that she never let me forget my gaffe. She took additional delight in telling others this story by pointing out that I was a psychologist who, presumably, was knowledgeable about communicating with other human beings. I never lived that story down even after this dear aunt went to the beyond.

I would not like to give the impression that the members of my conjugal or consanguineal family were uncultivated. Every so often, my parents would be invited to a soiree at the home of Signora and Signor D'Ambrosia. In their second-floor apartment on Eighteenth Avenue in Brooklyn, Signora D'Ambrosia would prevail upon her friends—professional musicians, singers and poets—to perform for her guests. After the concert, Italian cookies and black coffee were served. Without realizing it, on those Friday evenings, I was being exposed to the best in Italian culture, a culture I only later came to appreciate as extraordinarily rich in the arts. Apparently, my mother could soak up just so much culture, for there were evenings at the D'Ambrosias when she ended up in the kitchen playing pinochle and scopa with the men in the family.

Signora D'Ambrosia was short and round and carried herself with dignity, clearly a woman of refinement. Fluent in several languages, she spoke the Italian of her native Tuscany. She corrected my godmother's French assignments and also taught her to play the piano.

Her husband, whom she addressed affectionately as "Gigi," came from a fine, wealthy Italian family. Signor D'Ambrosia was also fluent in five languages. In Italy, this couple mixed with high society, but in coming to America, they were forced to a life of genteel poverty. From what my mother told me, this old-world couple had to leave Italy after Gigi fought a duel with a nobleman whose family sought revenge. The duel had to have been one with pistols, for I can't picture Signor D'Ambrosia, small in build, wielding a saber.

What I remember, too, about this unusual couple were the evenings Gigi would pay us one of his nocturnal visits. At eleven p.m., just about the time my parents and grandfather were winding down a game of cards, we would hear the bell ring. There, in the doorway, formally dressed in spats and sporting a silver-plated cane, was an aged gentleman. With a look of surprise, he would exclaim, "What! Have you forgotten?" What my parents had forgotten was the name of some obscure saint whose first name bore that of either my father or mother. Bemused by this nocturnal visitor who seemed to have been born in another century, my mother automatically brought out a tray of Italian delicacies which everyone feasted on so that no one would go to sleep hungry.

Soul food may be a term of current coinage but Italians have known for centuries what soul food means. Marcella Hazan has this to say: "Eating in Italy is one more manifestation of the Italians' age-old gift of making art out of life." From this perspective, my mother was an artist;

cooking for her was a labor of love. She knew intuitively that preparing delicious and wholesome meals was the most effective way of creating a rich family life. Eating together was a daily sharing of a common joy, a way of linking generations. The kitchen was the family hearth, a holy place.

Before describing the importance of having home cooked meals as daily fare when I was growing up, I feel the need to set the record straight about French and Italian cuisine. I cannot agree with that ebullient chef, Julia Child, in claiming French cooking as supreme among world cuisines. It is worth noting that in Arturo Baron's book, *Italians First* , he documents the fact that the first cookbook of the 'modern' world, written by Bartolomeo Sacchi, was published in Venice in 1475. The first health cookbook was written in 1614 by Giacomo Castelvetro under the title, *A Brief Account of the Fruits, Herbs and Vegetables of Italy*. Of course, it may be a sign of degeneracy among the American masses during the final years of the twentieth century that young and old alike have come to prefer Italian cuisine (not only pizza) over French. As for English cooking, Baron, the author and an English-born barrister whose parents emigrated from Naples, takes a side swipe at his countrymen by reminding them that the fork for dining was invented in Italy in the sixteenth century and came into use in England about 100 years later.

Some of my fondest recollections of being part of a large family are connected with our summer vacations. For a number of years, my family made the trip from Bay Ridge to Marlboro, in upstate New York, where the Chillura Brothers farm-resort was located. Before the New York Thruway was constructed, it took some four hours of driving to arrive at our destination. Besides packing clothing to last our family for two weeks, my mother prepared enough food for our trip so that, had we been stranded on a back road for a week, we could have survived without foraging. When we arrived at a particular lookout in the Catskills, out came a large basket containing a thermos of coffee, a container of milk, a dozen hard-boiled eggs, veal and pepper sandwiches, a large jar of pastina and a tin of biscotti, not to mention a variety of fruits and nuts. Everything but the refrigerator.

The East New York contingent of the family met us at The Big Apple Restaurant on Route 9W and, from this point on, we formed a caravan. After the parade of cars arrived in Marlboro, it was a short distance to the dirt road where a large wooden sign, designed in the form of an arch, marked our entryway. As we passed under the overhead trestle, all the car drivers began honking their horns. Their honking was not to announce that born-again Christians were on their way, but, another kind of good news: the musicians from Brooklyn had arrived. Our families were particularly welcomed to Chilluras since we supplied the entertainment and gave the resort zip.

Chilluras was an unpretentious resort, one of a number of small Italian places located in the "Bocce Circuit." Chilluras had its counterpart in other vacation enclaves such as the German Alps, The Emerald Isle, the Borscht Belt, and the Cuchifrito Circuit. At each ethnic resort enclave, Germans, Irish, Jews and Hispanics, not to overlook Ukrainians and African-Americans, congregated to enjoy themselves within the comfort and security of a culture that was familiar to them. It was like being at a home away from home. In one memorable photograph taken at Chilluras, I counted twenty-eight men, women and children, members of my family, all lined up across the lawn.

Recently, when I attended a program at the Albany Institute of History and Art titled *The Best of Both Worlds; Ethnic Resorts in the Catskills*, I came to appreciate the importance of these vacation places. People from different ethnic groups had more than one thing in common—they wanted to escape the summer heat in the city, to eat good food and plenty of it, to relax, and to be with others of their kind. These unique places to refresh body and soul have all but disappeared in the second half of the twentieth century. With families scattered across the United States, collective vacations with relatives have become infrequent. Family reunions are now in vogue.

Chilluras had one medium-size dining room with a seating capacity of well over a hundred people. There were fifteen rectangular tables that seated ten people each and three rectangular tables that seated twenty each. In the corner of the dining room, just off the kitchen, there was a piano that badly needed tuning. Though the wire-entwined backs to the chairs did not invite dallying with your meal, the quality of the cooking did.

The meals at Chilluras were wholesome and abundant. For breakfast, Mama Chillura made the rounds with a large basket of eggs timed to any taste. The creamy milk at each table had been refrigerated after the morning milking. The large slices of fresh crusty bread begged to be smeared with one-hundred-percent butter. At lunch and supper, the minestras and soups were laden with a variety of fresh vegetables and beans. I dare not dwell on the pasta and meat dishes lest I have an instant fat attack. As to cholesterol, that word had not yet found currency.

Indoors, above the dining room, were the bedrooms. Each family crowded into small rooms and made do. Out-of-doors, the uneven terrain was spotted with areas of dirt and grass. Off to the side of the main house was a swimming pool not much larger in size than one found, today, in a back yard in suburbia. Mothers, keeping a watchful eye over the children splashing in the pool, got caught up on the family news—who had just gotten engaged, who was going to have a baby, who had died.

Two tennis courts off to the side of the house were in a state of disrepair; not so, the two bocce courts. If it could be said that souls inhabit places, then you could identify the Italian soul in two places at Chilluras: the kitchen and the bocce courts. The long rectangular dirt enclosures where the men, never the women, played bocce were the scenes of heated exchanges and marvelous athletic feats. In the game of bocce, the idea is to get the large balls, rolled by members of your team, close to the small ball, the pallino. What was wondrous to behold was my father or uncle sending his ball into the air like a missile to knock out an opponent's ball that was "kissing" the pallino. When it came to a close decision as to which ball was closest to the pallino, someone stripped the branch of a bush to fashion a crude but effective measuring stick.

While the women gossiped and the men played bocce, the children roamed freely. First, there was a large barn where Pinto, the handyman, kept the cows. Pinto, a first-generation Italian-American who had grown up on a farm, welcomed the children with a broad, warm smile and invited us to touch the cows. Outside the barn, there were acres and acres of apple trees to climb, grape arbors and wild berry bushes to pick. A short distance from the barn was a small stream which opened into a small lake. As a young boy, it was a scary adventure to take the rowboat solo down the narrow winding stream. The only barrier preventing me from going over a small falls was a dilapidated wire mesh fence which I held on to for dear life.

Chilluras was a place where my father could relax. His impish side, normally concealed at home, was likely to surface when he was with his friend, Mr. Morani. In our family album, there is one photo of my father sitting on the diving board of the pool. He had donned an oversized brassiere that he had stuffed with towels. Next to him, Mr. Morani is reaching under one of my father's arms, shamelessly fondling the protuberances. Mr. Morani, a sculptor like my father, looked more the part of the sculptor, with his long face and pointed beard. His wife had the decorum of a woman like Eleanor Roosevelt. Their daughter was also a sculptor of sorts. In her profession as a plastic surgeon, she combined both her vocational and avocational skills which made her sought after in cases where limbs had been severed and bodies needed to be remodeled.

In addition to Chilluras, our families came together for outings to Staten Island, a borough of New York yet to be populated. Our caravan of cars boarded the ferry slip at Shore Road and 69th Street. As soon as the ferry pulled away from the dock, the children emptied out of the parked cars to stand at the steel gate at the front of the ferry boat. If the day was windy, the ocean spray on your face made you feel you were caught in a gentle rain. As the ferry drew close to the opposite shore, the children raced back to the automobiles. Once off the boat, our caravan of cars reformed to appear like the entourage at a gangster's funeral.

Arriving at a site in one of the state parks, the men started the fire while the women busied themselves setting up big pots in which to cook spaghetti, and setting tablecloths and eating utensils on the wooden tables. One delicacy, which was cooked over the fire, was roasted lamb. As if reenacting a primitive ritual, my grandfather and my uncle Joe circled the hearth playing mandolin and guitar while the roasting lamb released its pungent aromas. Whether the soul of the lamb was propitiated by the music and whether it knew that its sacrifice was for a good cause, a family celebration, is a question only the lamb can answer.

In recent years, I experienced the ebullient spirit of our family gathering at Casa Milanese, an Italian resort located near Modena, in upstate New York. Every two weeks, on Sunday, there is a dinner-dance which begins at 1:00 p.m. and lasts beyond 5:00 p.m. Whenever my wife and I go, in company with my cousin Vinny and his wife, I am flooded with sweet memories of growing up in Bay Ridge, Brooklyn, surrounded by "la famiglia."

The theme of a recent Sunday was "The Joy of Living." Delio Zani, our host, a cultured and impeccably dressed man, greeted guests at the door with genuine old-world charm. In the company of some two-hundred first- and second-generation Italian-Americans, most of whom would qualify as senior citizens, I felt quite at home.

The menu is the same for all the guests. On this particular Sunday of "La Gioia Di Vivere," the menu read: Antipasto (prosciutto, salami, Provolone); Coppa Tortellini in brodo (mini ravioli in chicken/beef broth); Tagliatelle alla Romangnole (pasta with tomato sauce); Veal Piccata (veal medallions in lemon/herb sauce). In addition, there were cooked vegetables, garden green salads and tomatoes. On each table, there was a bottle of Valpolicella red wine and Pinot Grigio white wine to further enhance the taste of the seven-course feast. For dessert, an

Italian cappuccino cake and cafe espresso (laced with a thimble of anisette) was served.

The music is always live, played on an electronic keyboard to the accompaniment of a guitar. With modern technology, the sound is that of a small band. The moment the musicians begin to play, there is a mass exodus from the dining tables to the dance floor. The duo plays up-tempo mazurkas and waltzes, a few foxtrots and rumbas, and toward mid-afternoon, they throw in a lively tarantella.

The tarantella is a traditional folk dance of southern Italy performed with a partner or solo. In the center of a ring of dancers, one dancer or a couple elevate their arms above their heads and innovate dance patterns with their feet, always maintaining dignified postures.

Given the Italian-American trait of adaptability, it is no surprise that when the band strikes up the Macarena and the Electric Slide, women and men alike are on the floor waving their arms and moving their legs in abandonment. As I watched the couples embrace doing waltzes, I had the sense that the men felt more manly, the woman more womanly, than is apparent in their modest displays of affection for each other off the dance floor.

But what makes the air more electric with excitement during the extended afternoon is the singing. On the dance floor, couples harmonize traditional songs, singing at the top of their lungs. They know the words to all the standard Italian melodies. The singing continues at the tables a capella when the band takes a break—the men sing in harmony the sweet, poignant melodies they heard their parents sing. What else would you expect of a nationality whose vocal brilliance includes Caruso and Pavarotti, Carlo Buti and Frank Sinatra?

Taking pride in their work, Italian-Americans have prospered over the generations, though there is little show of ostentation. At Casa Milanese, men follow a dress code by wearing jackets. The women dress attractively; there are no big mammas wearing black dresses. Well along in years, the men retain their strong builds, while the women are corseted, but are overweight only by American standards. When I look out at the dance floor, there is a lack of self-consciousness. The genius of a people is the simple, special talent to appreciate elemental pleasures like eating, singing and dancing, and turn them into something wonderful.

CHAPTER SIX

▼

NEIGHBORHOOD: AN ETHNIC MIX

If we didn't have Brooklyn, where would the other end of the bridge rest?

Phil Foster

Neighborhoods, like people, have souls; each has a unique character, even a destiny. The soul of Bay Ridge, Brooklyn, where I lived for the first thirty-three years of my life, is revealed through its unique history.

The origin of Bay Ridge dates back to 1652 when this southwestern tip of Brooklyn was purchased from the Nyack Indians by the Dutch West India Company. Bay Ridge was first called Yellow Hook by the early founders because of the color of the water on its shore when the sand of its hills washed into the bay. It was only much later, in 1853, that the present name was selected, a name which better describes this location with its beautiful bay and its ridge of hills.

Fort Hamilton is the oldest landmark in Bay Ridge. Named after Alexander Hamilton, the fort was built between 1825 and 1831 to protect New York Harbor from invasion by sea. It was at this site in 1776 that British and Hessian troops outflanked and defeated Washington's army in the Battle of Long Island.

This military installation served as a training ground for officers. The side of the fort which overlooked the Narrows had huge guns which could surface from underground. I thought of them as "disappearing guns." With this artillery, any vessel entering the Narrows could be blown out of the water. Though I romanticized seeing an enemy armada attempt to sneak through the Narrows on their way to destroy New York Harbor, I am glad I never saw my fantasy become a reality.

At the turn of this century, Bay Ridge began to change from land crossed by cow paths to a community of wealthy residential streets. My mother described the neighborhood when she first moved there as having nothing but "old-fashioned houses surrounded by empty lots." But even before my parents arrived when I was eighteen months old, the special status of Bay Ridge as a rural-suburban retreat had changed.

In 1915, the Fourth Avenue subway line was constructed. The 95th Street Station, located on 5th Avenue, one block from Fort Hamilton Parkway where I lived, is the last stop on the BMT for trains coming from Manhattan to Bay Ridge. Six blocks from the station is the Narrows, the passageway to the Atlantic Ocean for all ships coming from and going to Europe.

Fort Hamilton has given Bay Ridge a unique flavor. On the Fourth of July, in place of the Sunday afternoon polo matches in which the officers stationed at the military base competed, another kind of game was substituted, a simulated deadly game, a sham battle. In place of a dozen horses and riders thundering up and down the polo field in chase of a small ball, platoons of soldiers, outfitted with W.W.I battle gear, marched resolutely toward each other from opposite ends of the playing field. Affixed at the end of each soldier's rifle was a bayonet. Amidst the measured, staccato sound of machine gun fire were intermittent reports of rifle shots. As the troops advanced, one, then another soldier would drop in his tracks. Of course, I knew the bullets were fake, but the action seemed real.

As the cannons boomed and rifle fire increased in intensity, the high-pitched sound of a whistle pierced the air. It was the signal for the gas attack to begin. Soldiers donned their gas masks. With streams of gas swirling in the air, the combatants looked like aliens. The acrid smell of the smoke filled my nostrils, making it difficult to breathe. My eyes began to smart. Years later, during World War ll, I donned a gas mask as part of basic training. The memory of those mock battles staged at Fort Hamilton when I was a boy flooded back to me. I was no longer a spectator watching a military spectacle. I was one of the participants being trained for a military engagement which might, one day, become real.

During the summer months, at the sports arena located on the perimeter of the army base a block from my home, I watched wrestling and boxing. Tuesdays there were boxing bouts; Thursdays, wrestling matches. In the 1940s, when Joe Lewis and Jack Dempsey refereed a boxing match, the crowds overflowed. Some big-name wrestlers came to the arena, colorful performers like Gene "Mr. America" Stanley, "Baron" Michael Leone, "Tarzan" Frank Hewitt and "Jumping Joe" Savoldi.

These two sporting events drew fans from all over Brooklyn. Each week, crowds of boxing and wrestling devotees poured out of the subway station at 95th Street and headed for the arena. I positioned myself in the path of the oncoming crowds and sold bags of roasted peanuts I had obtained from a vendor. I did a brisk business; each ten-cent bag of peanuts netted me one penny. By the time the fans had disappeared into the arena, I had enough money to buy an ice cream soda with enough left over for candy bars. After finishing the soda and with the candy bars stuffed in my pockets, I crawled under the fence through a secret hole.

Once inside the arena, I sought a vantage point from which to watch the evening sports.

I preferred watching the wrestling matches because of the acrobatics and melodrama. In the ring, two men, each with the physique of a giant, bashed the other with fists and elbows, using his head for butting, his feet for stomping and his legs for squeezing his opponent's chest and stomach. Groans and cries filled the air as a hard-pressed wrestler tried to escape from a punishing hold. I could not understand how it was that these two grown men seemed to take great pleasure in inflicting pain on one another and even seemed to enjoy being punished. When one wrestler lifted his opponent off the mat, held him high overhead, then slammed his body down hard on the canvas, I winced. Recovering from this assault to his body, the enraged competitor turned himself into a human torpedo by bouncing off the ropes and ramming his head into the stomach of his adversary.

Nor was it only the two opponents who displayed histrionics worthy of silent screen actors. To heighten the drama, a wrestler would remonstrate with the referee and accuse him of incompetence and demand fair play. When anyone was foolhardy enough to make a threatening gesture toward "Gunner" Jackson after the referee had penalized him, that was the signal for all hell to break loose. The "Gunner," though visibly smaller than either of the contenders, lived up to his name and clobbered his accuser with cannon blows until the contesting wrestler turned craven. These side-show events between referee and wrestler brought cheers and jeers from the boisterous crowd of men and women. I cheered and jeered along with everyone else. What did I know?

One Thursday evening, I saw two oversized men walking down the sidewalk in my direction. I immediately recognized them as the two opponents I had seen in a wrestling match held the prior week. But here they were, walking arm in arm, as I had seen my uncles walk together. How could it be that these two hulks, barely able to stand side-by-side in the ring, were walking amicably together? I was certainly confused.

The next day, I asked our downstairs neighbor, Mr. Radice, a sports fan, how it was possible for two men to treat each other that way and still be friends. With a bemused smile, Mr. Radice told me that professional wrestling was faked for the most part, that it was entertainment rather than an authentic sport.

It would be years later, while doing research for a book about dance marathons, that I noted the similarities between this fad, which flourished during the twenties and thirties, and professional wrestling, which came decades later. Both combined sport with show business. What spectators wanted to see was a good show where the bad guys, who initially held the upper hand, were finally defeated by the good guys. What puzzled me about such forms of entertainment, then and now, is how audiences are willing not only to suspend disbelief, but reason as well.

Before the thirty-three-mile Belt Parkway, a road which stretched from Shore Road to the Bronx, opened on June 28, 1940, the shoreline of Fort Hamilton was wooded and picturesque, a great place to play cowboys and Indians. I would make a bow and arrow from the stalks of the tall bushes and imagine myself to be Sitting Bull. When I switched to being a cowboy, I brandished a gun I had constructed out of two pieces of wood formed like the number 7. I used two-inch squares of cardboard for ammunition to fire from a rubber band fastened to the gun barrel. Fort Hamilton, particularly during my childhood years, had an ambiance of the frontier.

Alongside the sea wall of the Narrows, I launched my first and last rowboat. The rowboat was constructed in the backyard of my home with the help of my friend Joseph Maresca. I thought we had created a nautical wonder. In this first endeavor as a ship builder, I encountered a number of challenges: how to curve leftover planks of wood and how to make the boat watertight. When we finished, the result was clearly not a thing of beauty. None-the-less, to me, building this boat was a singular achievement which made me feel proud.

Joe and I carried the boat down to the shore wall. My joy knew no bounds as I anticipated taking my first ride. However, given the heavy weight of the boat and the crude construction—we had used tar to fill in the cracks between the boards—you might guess what happened. We put the boat in the water and before we could properly christen it with a bottle of Pepsi, the rowboat began to fill and slowly sink before our eyes. Soon, it disappeared altogether, even before I had a chance to christen it "The Balboa," after Italo Balboa, an Italian aviator who had recently caused a stir flying a sea plane from Europe to New York.

It was on the site of my maritime disaster that, years later, the Verrazzano Bridge was constructed. My mother spent hours leaning out of the second-story window of our home watching the huge structure taking shape. Perhaps the reason for her long vigil was that she was in a state of trance. She seemed mesmerized watching a small treadle, like some mechanical spider, weaving strands of cable as it went back and forth, back and forth, from Brooklyn to Staten Island.

The Verrazzano Bridge was named after the Florentine navigator Giovanni da Verrazzano who, like Columbus, started out for the Orient and ended up elsewhere. Verrazzano discovered New York and the Narragansett Bays in 1542. Not everyone was happy to see the bridge constructed. Some four-hundred families in Brooklyn living near the site lost their homes in order to clear space for the approach to the bridge.

Bay Ridge was a place where the life of the spirit was affirmed in many places of worship: St. Patrick's Church, the Norwegian Methodist Church, the Jewish synagogue and the Greek Orthodox Church, to name a few. But you could also identify the life of the soul by the ethnic places that nourished the soul through the body.

Should you crave a delicious potato salad, or a succulent roast beef sandwich, there was Freudens, a delicatessen run by Norwegian-Americans. For the longest time, Bay Ridge was the location of the largest Scandinavian community in the United States. Next door to Freudens was DiNatales, an Italian grocery store where the fruits and vegetables were always fresh and abundant. German-Americans ran an ice-cream parlor in which you drank malted milk from glasses set in metal holders. Late at night, after seeing a double feature at the Harbor Theater, I looked forward to a dish of creamy rice pudding at the Greek diner across from the theater. Around the corner from my home was a Mom and Pop store owned by the Cohens where I could roll my eyes to the back of my head after tasting an egg cream soda. After I came of age, if I was really thirsty, there was Gray's Irish Tavern at the corner of the block.

When we first moved to Bay Ridge, almost everything was delivered to your door steps. A large man with frightening tongs and a leather apron delivered ice for the kitchen ice box. The coal man ran a ton of coal down a chute into the basement. Baked goods, bread, groceries and fruits, milk, even fresh fish, came to our door step. Every so often, the sound of a gong from a small truck let you know that the man who sharpened knives and scissors was in the neighborhood. Music to my ears was the tinkling bell of the Good Humor man who held out the promise of a free popsicle if you were fortunate enough to get the Lucky Stick.

There were still others who came directly to our home. The Fuller Brush Man sold quality housecleaning implements and offered a small brush as a free sample. Every week, the man from the Metropolitan Insurance Company diligently made his rounds to collect whatever a family could afford, even a half dollar during the hard times of the Great Depression.

There were some special food staples, however, that were not home delivered, but these provisions required only a ten-minute drive. Located on 18th Avenue and 86th Street, there was an enclave of Italians with their own special pastry shop and a deli. Scoppas pastries were worth the trip alone. For Christmas or Easter, or for a special occasion such as a birthday or an anniversary, my mother's first stop was Scoppas. Each time we entered the store with its aromatic smells, I was placed in a dilemma. Should I go for the cannoli with the white cream,

or the pasticiotti with yellow cream? To make choosing even more difficult, there were crispy sfogliatelli with a filling made from grain and
cream cheese. And on hot summer evenings, a trip to Scoppas included
real lemon ice. What a treat!

The Mangeracina Deli sold fresh ricotta, mozzarella and provolone
cheeses, prosciutto and other Italian delicacies. In the 20s and 30s, these
staples were largely unknown to the general public, but are now household words. Unfortunately, with our craze to reduce cholesterol and
blood pressure, I have come to regard all of the above delicacies as suspect
foods unless they are skimmed and trimmed. As a result, something precious has been lost so that I might live a few extra years. I know that I am
doing damage to my soul for the sake of my body.

On the same side of the street as Scoppas and Mangeracinas, there
was a chicken market. Unlike the savory smells that came from the pastry
shop and delicatessen, as you entered the chicken market, a cavernous
building, it smelled and sounded like a barn. In crate after crate were
live chickens milling around and clucking. The butcher would reach
into a cage, pull out a chicken and cut its throat right before your eyes.
He flopped the chicken in a funnel, head down, to let the blood run out
into a barrel. Next he dipped the chicken into a barrel of boiling water
and plucked its feathers. There was no question in my mother's mind
about having a fresh chicken for our supper that night. Only later, when
I told a friend of mine about this experience, did I learn that his Jewish-
American mother bought poultry the same way.

Once at home with the bounty, my mother would prepare the
chicken using her special recipe for "Chicken ala Cacciatore." First, she
sauteed the chicken with garlic in olive oil, adding salt, oregano and a
few bay leaves. When the chicken was almost cooked, she added onions
and then balsamic vinegar and allowed time for the chicken to simmer.
Sopping the gravy with fresh Italian bread and drinking a glass of
homemade red wine I knew the meaning of ambrosia even before I
could spell it. A word of caution to the uninitiated; this Italian speciality,

when served in a restaurant, is made with a tomato sauce and has a very different taste. Should I gain admittance to Heaven, Chicken ala Cacciatore, the way my mother prepared it, had better be available or else I am out of there.

Three small bedrooms, a kitchen, a dining room and a living room met the basic needs of our growing family. Before my younger brother and sister were born, I shared a bedroom with my older sister; the other bedroom was for my grandfather. When the family grew to four children, my parents built a room in the basement for my grandfather. Over the years, my brother and I came to share one bedroom while my two sisters shared another bedroom.

I don't ever remember feeling cramped or uncomfortable in this house, though when I revisited it years later, I was amazed to see how small the rooms actually were compared to their size in my mind's eye. The rooms may have been small, but the life lived in them was large.

In front of our house, below the porch, was a small flower garden with a magnolia planted in the center. Looking back at old photos, I can trace the passage of the years by the growth of this gift of nature. Magically, each year, the magnolia tree blossomed around Easter Sunday, its white and pink blossoms resplendent with color and fragrance. Many years later, in a college course on mythology, I learned that the magnolia is a pagan reminder of spring as a time of renewal. Our magnolia tree also served a secular function. It was a colorful backdrop for my two sisters posing for a picture in their new Easter bonnets.

The backyard, alongside the two-car garage, had a long, narrow garden fenced in from our neighbor's lot next door. In our neighborhood, many Italians who came from southern Italy planted a vegetable and fruit garden. In our's, on either side of the two narrow strips of land, there were several fig trees. At the far end of the garden was a small grape arbor which yielded bunches of concord grapes purple to the eye and tart to the taste. Among the vegetables grown in our garden you could find tomatoes, peppers, scallions, lettuce, zucchini, parsley and basilica.

My favorite summer lunch was (and still is) a salad made with tomatoes, fresh basil, garlic, red onions, oregano and olive oil. Dipping a crusty piece of fresh Italian bread into the juice of this salad I was in heaven. If this salad were served at the evening meal, it would be accompanied by a glass of homemade dry white wine and my life, at that moment, would be complete.

Extending over our garage was a giant apricot tree which belonged to our neighbor, Mr. Orlando. By climbing the trestle in my grandfather's grape arbor, it was easy to swing up onto the roof of the garage and, from there, climb the apricot tree. The tree grew on the property of Mr. Orlando, an irascible first-generation Italian-American. Each time he caught me perched on one of the tree branches, he made wild gestures with his arms and hands signaling me to get off his property, even threatening to call the police. With this warning, I would scramble out of the tree, down the grape trestle and, when the coast was clear, I would return to my tree hideout. Perched on the garage roof, by attaching a rope to one of the lower branches and by pulling on the rope, I could gain a clear view of our backyard without myself being seen. If my sister and her girlfriends were playing down below, I could not resist taking out my slingshot and, with apricot pits as ammunition, pelting the unsuspecting group at play.

Every autumn, our cellar, before it became a finished basement, was redolent with the smell of grapes. The ritual of making wine would begin with the arrival of the truck which delivered boxes and boxes of grapes to our backyard. As a boy not yet ten, my job was to pry open the wooden boxes and, after the grapes had been put in the press, to break the boxes for firewood. Being a participant-observer in the winemaking process, I came to appreciate both the art and science of the vintner. My father and grandfather, as well as all of my uncles, made wine, and each boasted that his was the best. They are all dead now and each took his secret formula to the grave.

My taste for wine started at an early age. One evening when I was not yet five, I went down to the cellar and opened the spigot of one or our wine barrels. I don't know how much wine I drank or how much wine was lost. Had I received some strong potches on my behind, they had been well deserved.

If there is any agreement among first- and second-generation Italian-Americans, it is the importance, no, the necessity of drinking wine with their meals. One Italian proverb goes: "A day without wine is a day without sun." Although the image of bread and wine as a symbol of the body and blood of Christ doesn't quite stir my spirit, I must concede that drinking homemade wine at dinner is a sacred ritual. When the poet in "The Rubiyat of Omar Kayam" sits under a tree with a jug of wine and a loaf of bread and toasts his lady-love, I regard his action a consecration.

On the subject of homemade wine, I realize that what I am about to say is irrational and borders on the absurd. But bear with me if you would understand my uncontrolled passion, particularly for homemade muscatel wine. No, not the muscatel wine you purchase in a wine or liquor store that tastes sweet and lacks body. What I am talking about is a dry white wine that has a unique flavor and bouquet and packs a wallop.

Even today, should I hear of anyone making homemade muscatel wine, I will stop just short of making the wine-maker an offer he can't refuse, should he deny my polite entreaty as I kiss him on both cheeks. You may be familiar with the etiquette and protocol of sharing the fruits of the vine among Italians. You pay a relative or friend a visit and you will be generously rewarded by your host who will fill and refill your glass until, reeling in your chair, you finally say, "Basta!". But he will rarely give you a bottle to take home, much less sell you a bottle should you be so insensitive as to offer to pay him.

In light of the delicate protocol related to procuring homemade wine, I had entertained the idea of indenturing my children to a wine-maker and accepting wine for wages. In that addictive frame of mind, I made it clear to my children that unless they married into the home of a wine maker, I would refuse consent. Let me add that I was ashamed of having such bizarre fantasies but, finally, the truth is out in the open.

I honor Dionysus but acknowledge his power. Should I drink wine at the noon meal, I can count on spending the rest of the day in lethargy and torpor. Drinking wine without the accompaniment of food makes me dizzy. Furthermore, the two characteristics associated with this deity, wine and dance, do not work well for me. At dinner dances, when I have been fortified with a liberal amount of wine, my wife informs me that my lead is so rough she would rather grapple with a dancing bear. Were I performing an infamous Apache Dance, where I would have license to manhandle my partner as part of the act, I might indulge my taste for the fruits of the vine before stepping out on the dance floor. But aware that in the retinue of Dionysus are the dreaded Furies, I wisely forego the pleasures of the cup to avoid my partner's displeasure and retribution.

Growing up in Bay Ridge, there were two signs that I had walked into the right house when I returned home from school. One sign was the sound of music coming from an Italian radio station or from the record player. Caruso was the Pavarotti of his day, but it was Carlo Buti, crooning a Neapolitan love song, that brought sweetness to the Italian soul.

The other way to tell I was home, should I have suffered temporary amnesia, was through my nose. If there was no aroma of garlic and onions being sauteed in preparation for the tomato sauce, I definitely knew I was in the wrong place. By the time I entered the kitchen where my mother spent much of her time, I was salivating like one of Pavlov's dogs.

Though no one ever verbalized it in so many words, eating together as a family took on the importance of a sacred ritual. Our kitchen and dining room table were symbolic of the good things connected with family life. All the important events were celebrated around the dinner table: birthdays, marriages, even funerals, and, of course, all the holidays. Every Christmas Eve, the traditional dish was "bacala," dry salted cod fish that had to be soaked for 3 days to remove the salt. Once desalted, it was either cooked in tomato sauce with spicy black olives and leeks, or pan-fried in a light batter to a crisp. This is one Christmas Eve tradition that we uphold in my family to the present day.

For me, eating served many needs beyond physical nourishment. When frustrated, I raided the Frigidaire (I thought everyone kept their food in Frigidaires; only later, did I find out that the proper generic name was refrigerator). Angry, happy, or sad, I raided the Frigidaire.

Of course, food to an Italian parent could become an obsession as it was to my uncle who insisted that you eat your zucchini whether you liked it or not. Watching one of my oversized aunts sit between her two daughters at the supper table was better than a Chaplin comedy. This aunt would turn to her anemic-looking daughter and implore her, "Eat, for God's sake, eat!" Then, she would wheel around to her rotund daughter who was stuffing her mouth, and cuff her on the head screaming, "For the love of the Virgin Mary, stop eating!"

My mother was generally acknowledged to be one of the better cooks in our extended family. After my marriage, during the year we lived at my parents' home, my wife apprenticed herself to my mother to glean her culinary secrets. It was during that year that I committed a major blunder. One evening at the supper table I blurted out to my mother, "What did you put in the meatballs?" My outburst was followed by a deadly silence. Cued by my mother's stern look, I became aware that my wife's eyes had began to tear. In an instant, I realized how I had put my foot in my mouth. It was my wife, not my mother, who had put Romano cheese instead of locatelli cheese in the meatballs that made the difference.

My macho pride prevented me from immediately getting down on my knees, on the spot, and begging forgiveness. Needless to say, when we retired for the night, there were no good-night kisses. The following day, I sought to make amends and played with the idea of buying her a mink coat or a Mercedes-Benz. Not that she would have been bought off with such gifts, even if I had had the money. Never one to bear grudges, she soon forgave me. Forever after, even on the rare occasion that she has cooked something not to my liking, or used cilantro to spice up the dish (a condiment to which I have the greatest antipathy and can detect its presence even in the most infinitesimal amounts), I lavish her with praise and have been eating well ever since.

Peasant fare, like minestras made from escarole and potatoes, or pasta and beans for everyday meals was one thing. But Sunday dinners when we had company were something else. Cooking started early in the morning. By the time early afternoon came around, a six- or seven-course extravaganza was ready: antipasto; chicken soup with pastina and small meatballs; pasta with sausage; chicken a la cacciatore; mixed salads with fennel.

After the meal, out came the hot chestnuts, fruits and my favorite pastries—cannoli and sfoglatelli. To complete the meal, there was espresso with anisette and a twist of lemon peel. Mind you, this was not Christmas or Thanksgiving dinner, but a feast that happened at least once a month. One of my favorites to end an everyday meal was sliced fresh peaches in red wine; at the end of a Sunday feast, there was the supreme dessert, the indescribable taste of cherries long-soaked in a liqueur which my mother had prepared in jars when cherries were in season.

The days of seven-course dinners ended with my parents' generation. It is hard to believe that we relished such quantities of food. I don't remember anyone ever having a stomach upset that a glass of Brioschi didn't remedy. If the quantity of food consumed has changed, the quality of Italian cooking in my family has not been totally lost. The old recipes get trotted out occasionally even as chicken and turkey have supplanted sausage and veal. Of course, fettucini alfredo, one of my favorites, heads the list of Taboo Foods.

Nor has all the precious folklore related to food been lost with our third-generation offsprings. Mark, our "Italian Son," whose childhood photos show him happily stuffing his mouth with spaghetti, carries on some of the old traditions, especially regarding food and its preparation. On our all-too-infrequent visits to the north country where he and his family live, I can count on a feast my son will prepare: fettucini ala carbonara, risotto ala Milanese and pasta ala putanesca. I don't believe this last recipe was passed down from mother to son since the word "putanesca" is descriptive of the meal prepared in a brothel for the paying customers. It is a recipe that can be prepared in a short time to fortify the staying power of ardent guests who might want to dally in a house that seeks to satisfy carnal pleasure.

When my father died and my older sister moved to be closer to her daughter in New Jersey, my mother sold the house and went to live with my sister. Many years after she had moved, I had a strong urge to go back to see the house in which I had grown up. What I observed when I returned, both in my parents' home and in the neighborhood, was disquieting.

Anticipating resistance from the current homeowner to a stranger coming to the door asking if he might walk through the house, I took with me several photographs of the house that had been taken when I lived there. A young man answered the bell; after a brief introduction, I handed him the photos. He informed me that the house had been converted into a doctor's office. The first floor was divided into a series of cubicles. Since no was at home in the upper floor, I was unable to see the remainder of the house nor did I to ask permission to go down to the basement where the young man and his wife had their living quarters.

It was disheartening to see all the windows of the first floor barred. In the small landing between my house and the house next door stood an iron fence where once had been open space. Surrounding the small garden where colorful flowers once grew were formidable iron rings. The magnificent magnolia tree in the front garden, which miraculously bloomed every Easter, was gone. The large cement flower vase which rested on one corner of the porch was broken and only a jagged base remained.

In the backyard, the vegetable and fruit garden my parents had tended was blacktopped. In the middle of the driveway, in large block script letters, set in stone, were the initials M.D.; alongside the initials was the date the house was purchased. Placing this information with such finality in such a location, where it could not be readily seen by anyone, puzzled me. Perhaps it was a marker to help the occupants feel reassured that their ancestral gods from the Philippine Islands would know where to locate them.

Despite the changes that had taken place in my parents' home, the remaining houses on the block appeared the same as I remembered. It was a shock to find that the corner property which once housed Gray's Tavern, a friendly place where my grandfather would go to buy a pail of beer, was now the location of Perry's Fine Rifles and Shotgun Shop, which sold firearms and issued New York State hunting licenses.

On the day of my visit, I looked across the street and observed a few mothers with their children in a park playground. The park benches had been heavily initialed and were in need of repair. On the cement near one of the benches was a broken bottle. Behind the park was the roadway leading up to the Verrazzano Bridge.

Though there had been many changes, my old neighborhood remained recognizable. The library on the corner of 4th Avenue was still there. The small park on Shore Road was intact, though it is now dwarfed by the massive Verrazzano Bridge which looms alongside it. The twenty-foot monument dedicated to the Dover Patrol, an American naval force sent to Europe during W.W.I, built with funds from grateful people in Great Britain who appreciated America's help, is still there. Squeezed into a corner of the park is the cannon with the massive balls that I climbed upon as a boy. I wondered then and wonder now how this weapon could have shot those massive cannon balls.

Two medical buildings have been erected near the park on Shore Road to meet the needs of the burgeoning number of elderly people living there. The Harbor Theater and the Greek restaurant across the street, both landmarks in my memory, are gone. Bay Ridge retains some of its original European ethnic flavor and has added Latinos, Asians and African-Americans to the mix. Part of the change is reflected in the food that is now available at take-out places and restaurants. In place of restaurants which served the traditional menu of pasta dishes from southern Italy, I found one that specialized in northern Italian cuisine.

In earlier days, I rode the trolley car, with its sparking overhead electrical lines, to reach the shopping center at 86th street. Upon revisiting the neighborhood, I rode a bus to get to my destination. Soon after I climbed aboard, a man in his fifties, quite drunk, paid his fare and staggered down the aisle to fall into a seat. He was immediately followed by a young woman in her early twenties who hoisted a can of beer in the air as she directed a barrage of curses at the man who preceded her. Her hands unsteady, she spilled some beer on the bus seat and proceeded to demand that her father pay her fare. His adamant refusal prompted the bus driver to stop his vehicle and eject the daughter. Bearing witness to this scene, I thought about father-daughter relationships in a bygone era. Given the tight structure that existed within the Irish, Italian and Greek families who lived in Bay Ridge decades ago, a scene such as this would have been unthinkable. On the second floor of a building on 4th Avenue and 86th Street, near the barber shop where I once had my hair cut, there is a prominent sign in the window: "Bridge Back To Life Counseling."

The Christening: My godmother (seated on the left); my godfather (with the tall hair holding my cousin); my earth mother, earth father, and sister. I'm in the middle with the Teddy bear.

My Family: My father (left), mother and brother (center), my grandfather (right), my sister (right) and me(left)

My Relatives: Uncle Joe brings in a surprise dish (probably baby octopus) at a family celebration. Uncle Tom is up to no good seated next to my great Aunt Francischina.

The Clan: Vacationing at Chillura Brother's Farm and Resort in the Catskills. I'm in the center, in my first pair of long pants.

The Hulk: Me as a teenager loose in Coney Island

The Great Event: How lucky can one man be?

50ᵗʰ Wedding Anniversary: My parents rounding out the years.

Champagne Contest: A Friday night at the Nevele Resort, flanked by women. The Army was never like this!

The Lesson: Professor Long-Hair in Union College's Jackson Gardens, doing his thing.

Family Reunion: Sons and daughters, their spouses and offspring (more came later) on the deck of our home overlooking our Japanese Garden. Brother Ernie, shortly before he passed away, is on the left.

CHAPTER SEVEN

▼

First Love and No Longer Innocent

Love thy neighbor, even when he plays the trombone.

Jewish Proverb

Irish and Italian families lived alongside each other on Fort Hamilton Parkway between 94th and 95th Streets, where we lived. Most of our neighbors were first- and second-generation Americans. The Crawfords were Irish and impressed me with their smarts; I thought they must have been direct descendants of the Pilgrims. They rented the first-floor apartment of my parents' home. Mrs. Crawford took my mother in hand and schooled her in the American way.

Mrs. Crawford worked for the Bell Telephone Company and always seemed brash and self-assured. I am convinced that in her youth she danced the Charleston with unrestrained vigor and drank bathtub gin from a small flask tucked under her garter belt. She became my mother's closest friend. She taught her to smoke and play bridge to help her relax while bringing up a family of four children. True, my mother's mentor taught her vices, but she also contacted social service agencies who supplied us with food and clothing during the hard times of the Great Depression.

Smoking did seem to help my mother to be less tense. Some thirty years later, she had a heart attack and quit smoking on the doctor's orders. If it could be said that there was anything of value in my mother's smoking habit, it would be that, luckily, none of her children ever smoked.

I remember when I was not yet five years old picking up a lighted butt from the pavement and putting it in my mouth. As I inhaled, I nearly choked to death. That was the first and last time I tried smoking a cigarette. In my early twenties, I did make an attempt to smoke a pipe. Having a pipe in my hand made me feel debonair and world wise; besides, I liked the smell of the aromatic tobacco. What I didn't like was the bitter aftertaste and how my clothes reeked of smoke afterwards. I soon abandoned that habit and attempted to shore up my shaky self-image by taking to the dance floor.

The Crawfords were a study in contrasts. While Mrs. Crawford was forward in her behavior, her husband was reserved most of the time. After downing several whiskies at one of our house parties, Mr. Crawford's alter ego would take over. He would begin to howl like a lone wolf in the wilderness as he tried to carry an Irish tune off-key. His performance reduced my father to helpless laughter.

Mr. Crawford was a detective, but his appearance and demeanor gave little indication of what he did for a living. He neither acted nor looked like Sam Spade in a Dashiell Hammett mystery novel, nor Humphrey

Bogart in *The Maltese Falcon.* Whenever I met Mr. Crawford, he was always meticulously dressed, a real Irish dandy. I could only assume that the detective work he was called upon to do was investigating insurance claims; I don't see how he could have dealt with a real thug.

The Radices were our next tenants. Mr. Radice, a second-generation Italian-American, was an electrician by trade and a self-styled historian. He held strong opinions about politics and politicians and, though he identified himself as a Democrat, he regarded President Franklin D. Roosevelt as an authoritarian blue blood, a dictator. Mr. Radice viewed himself as one-hundred-percent American, a union man and a loyal fan of the Brooklyn Dodgers. His mother was the prototype of the aging Italian mamma, perpetually ailing and always clothed in a black dress which ballooned around her. Both his mother and uncle lived with the family. His uncle, whom everyone called Chi-Chick, had a nervous habit. In conversation, he would forever jingle a pant's pocket full of nickels while chewing a jaw full of tobacco. Every day, when the season began, he jingled his coins as he headed to the subway which would take him to the race track.

Mrs. Radice's immigrant parents came from Hungary. I always addressed her as "Signora" out of respect. She had a pleasant disposition compared to her husband. On a few occasions, she consented to play the zither, an instrument that I had never before seen or heard.

The Radices had three daughters. Nettie, the oldest, was my first love. How sweet it was on a balmy summer evening to be with her on our front porch talking and kidding around. Our relationship never became a torrid love affair, for I don't even remember holding her hand. The only time I actually had an opportunity to kiss her was at a neighborhood party when we played spin-the-bottle.

Our puppy-love relationship lasted a few summers and ended when she met another second-generation American-Italian who was more experienced with girls than I was. I felt jealous and hurt. In later years, I learned that after she married, my dream girl's alluring figure had given way to one that resembled her mother's. Mrs. Radice had a stocky build and what the kids on the block irreverently called "piano legs."

Our house was attached on the left side to a duplex red-brick dwelling. The left side of the duplex was occupied by Jack and Bridie Mars, both born in Ireland. Besides their three sturdy sons, who were always ready to help my parents, the Marses had a mentally retarded daughter. Watching her grow from a girl to a young woman while her behavior continued to be that of a child was distressing.

The couple who lived above the Marses was strange. Mr. Luria was a house painter and always looked and smelled as if he had just come off the job, while his wife was always made up and dressed as if she were going to a fashion show. Despite her outward appearance, she had the sex appeal of a siren in a wax museum.

Across the alley from the Marses lived Tony and Monie Gato. Italian and Irish, the Gatos had four children, all boys. Monie, not yet in her forties, fell out of her second-story window and died. After Monie's death, Tony was a broken man.

Next door to the Gatos lived the De Lorenzo family. Besides the two brothers, Victor and Frank, markedly different from each other—one gregarious, the other a near recluse—there were two sisters, Marilyn and Lydia. In my early twenties, I was strongly attracted to Marilyn, who was athletic and wholesome-looking. When her dates arrived in their sports cars equipped with outdoor rumble-seats, I fantasized that it was me in the car with Marilyn. Lydia was the princess type. Her fiancé, a branch manager of the Fuller Brush Company, arrived at the door in his Cadillac.

Farther down the block was the Marinello family. Mrs. Marinello was a cousin of Mrs. Radice. The Marinellos had three daughters and a son. Dark-skinned Betty, the oldest of their three girls, had a crush on me, but my heart was committed to her cousin, Nettie, who had a fair complexion. Years after I left the neighborhood, I heard that Danny, the Marinello's son, received his medical degree at the University of

Bologna and became a doctor. During the fifties, of the dozen medical schools in Europe and England recognized by the American Medical Association, all but three were located in Italy.

Next door to the Marinello family were the DeMarias. Tessie, my older sister's girlfriend, was a seductress, though I don't think she intended to be. Once, when I went with my sister to visit Tessie, I became greatly excited when she appeared before us in her slip through which I could see her bra and panties. Her alluring figure, like that of Mrs. Luria, gave my imagination many erotic twists and turns. If Tessie struck me as an Egyptian princess, her sister, Tee-Tina, reminded me of the Witch in *Hansel and Gretel*. The DeMaria brothers, Gino and Joey, like the DeLorenzo boys, were also a study in contrasts. Gino was tall and fair; if he were Spanish, he might have been a Castellian, a bull-fighter or a flamenco dancer. Joey was short and swarthy and would have easily passed for a Spanish gypsy.

It was Joey, a half-dozen years older than me, who first put me straight about sex. In addition, under the guise of teaching me how to box, he pummeled the hell out of me. He also introduced me to BB gun fights. I shudder to think how I might have lost an eye in this boys' game.

Farther down the block were two Irish families. At the corner of 95th Street and Fort Hamilton Parkway was a tavern owned by Mr. Kelly, an Irishman to the hilt. On hot summer evenings, my father, Mr. Radice, Mr. DeMaria and my uncle Pep played cards at the kitchen table. They bet small amounts of money in games of briscola and tre sete. At the end of the evening, the money in the kitty was used to buy a large pail of beer. They would send my grandfather to Mr. Kelly's bar to make the purchase. Mr. Kelly always treated my grandfather (he called him "Uncle Mike," as did others outside the family) to a beer at the bar. It is more than likely that when my grandfather made his return trip with the pail of beer, he fortified himself additionally along the way.

My grandfather's arrival with the beer signaled the real fun of the evening: the game of "Padrone" and "Sotto." The winners were the

"Padrones" and decided who among the losers, the "Sottos," would get a glass of beer. A padrone would say to his partner, "Let's give DeMaria a drink," but his partner might raise some objection, in which case Mr. DeMaria was left to lick his dry lips. In the end, everyone got a glass of beer but, noting the expressions on the faces of those who were initially refused a drink, I imagined future vendettas in the making.

One Norwegian family rented the apartment in my parents' home after I left for the service. When I returned home for a furlough, I learned from my mother about the noisy flare-ups between husband and wife in the apartment below. My mother was tempted more than once to intervene when she heard angry shouts and cries. The next day, traces of black and blue on the face of Mrs. Larson confirmed my mother's suspicions that there had been domestic violence. But calm followed storm, and when my mother came to realize that our tenants were decent people except for these periodic outbreaks, she kept her counsel. Besides, she never knew who was to blame for these outbursts, for the husband drank periodically and the wife had the tongue of a shrew.

In addition to memories I have of the families who lived on our block, what I recall with most vividness from my early years were my experiences related to sex. Sex was something my parents never talked about. As an altar boy at St. Patrick's Church, it was unthinkable to ask any nun or priest for information about sexuality. "Playing Doctor," examining how the girls I played with were different from me, did satisfy my curiosity, but as to where babies came from, I didn't have a clue.

I was innocent in other ways. Like most children, I believed there was a Santa Claus whose primary function was to bring me toys on Christmas Eve. I can still see, as if it were right before my eyes, the large red wagon I received one Christmas when I was six years old. But, at some indeterminate time in my childhood, I stopped believing and I can't recall what changed my mind. It didn't bother me in the least that Santa Claus, with his roly-poly figure and his large bag of toys, should never have been able to fit down the narrow chimney in our living room. I don't remember anyone coming right out and saying, "Hey, bambino, there is no Santa Claus. Sorry!" And the same is true of the Tooth Fairy. What a great feeling it was to reach under my pillow the day after I had lost a tooth and find a quarter. Pure enchantment! What a price to pay to grow up.

In my early teens, my education in erotica took a giant step forward when Anna Campanella, who lived around the block from my home, invited me to one of her parties. I had no problem socializing, gulping down the soda and eating popcorn and cookies. But when it came to the games that followed, I was not on sure ground. We played "Spin the Bottle," and when it was my turn to kiss, I was uncertain what to do with my protruding nose, whether to turn my head to the left or to the right. There was another problem: Should I keep my eyes open or closed when I kissed a girl? Out of embarrassment, I opted for closing my eyes. My fear was that if I kept my eyes open, counting the pimples on my partner's cheek would have cooled my adolescent ardor.

From my early Catholic upbringing, I sensed that kissing a girl with my lips apart was well beyond committing a venial sin and clearly in the direction of a mortal sin. I never did get a definitive reading of this matter of open and closed mouth kissing from any Catholic source. The lyrics of *As Time Goes By* in the film *Casablanca* still says it all: "A kiss is still a kiss!"

Besides indoor games like "Spin the Bottle," there was a variety of outdoor games we played. "Kick the Can" comes readily to mind. Two teams are pitted against each other. When Team A is up, the members of Team B scatter and find hiding places near home base, located in a central place on the neighborhood block. If you are discovered in your hiding place, you are brought to the area designated as home base. The idea is for one of your teammates to free you by kicking the can before the den keeper captures the rescuer. When everyone on one team is captured, the other side has the opportunity to hide. This was a unisex game, though that word had not yet been invented.

Another game, "Buck, Buck, How Many Horns Are Up?" (also referred to as "Johnny on a Pony"), was a boy's game. One team lined up in a row; each member bent over and tucked his head under the legs of the teammate before him. The "pillow" leaned against the wall at the head of the line of bodies which came to resemble a giant centipede. The members of the other team, one by one, jumped and landed on the chain of bodies, always taking care to leave room behind him for the rest of his teammates to pile on. When all the team had leaped into place, the team captain held up his fingers and yelled, "Buck, Buck, how many horns are up?" If the opposing team captain guessed correctly, the teams changed position. Not a game for sissies or for the mixing of the sexes.

Before the advent of television and formalized sports, street games went on at all times of the day. In "Stoop Ball," the idea was to hit the ball off the corner of the step and see if anyone could catch it before it hit the ground. In "Punch Ball," you held a soft, pink Spaulding ball in one hand, and hit it with the fist of your other hand. Unlike in baseball, where you hit the ball with a bat, you could very accurately aim and place the ball with your hand. In "Stick Ball," you did use a bat, usually a sawed-off broom handle.

In my late teens and early twenties, my favorite game was handball, played against a wall. Saturday afternoons and Sunday mornings after church, I went to the school yard to play. I am right-handed and had a very effective "kill" shot—I would hit the ball very low on the baseboard, which made it difficult, if not impossible, for my opponent to return it. My weakness, however, was an underdeveloped left hand, which prevented me from becoming a neighborhood champ. To this day, several fingers of my right hand are puffed up larger than those on my left, and the middle finger of my right hand is curved out of shape, vestiges of slamming my hand and fingers against the side of a four-walled handball court.

For winter sport, with my American Flyer in hand, I waited at the bottom of a steep hill for a car to turn the corner. My right hand holding the sled parallel to the road, I grabbed the back bumper of the moving vehicle with my left hand, then plopped down on the sled and let the car take me to the top of the hill. Nearing the top of the hill, I would steer to a snowbank to avoid traffic on the main avenue. Some motorists became annoyed if you tried to hitch on to their car and would stop, get out and utter threats, or they kept driving but would attempt to throw you off the bumper by weaving from one side of the road to the other. How I didn't dislocate a shoulder or have a serious accident, I don't know. However maniacal riding car bumpers was, I never tried hitching on to a trolley car as some of my friends did, which was suicidal.

In my mid-teens, I attempted to shore up my self-confidence through body-building and giving myself positive auto-suggestions. When I read about Emile Coue and his system of "Self-Mastery by Auto-Suggestion," I began repeating his famous sentence: "Day by day, in every way, I am getting better and better." Monsieur Coue, a pharmacist turned healer, held the momentary attention of the American people during the twenties with his one-sentence nostrum. To set the record straight about his being a charlatan, he said, "I am not a miracle man. I do not heal people. I teach them to cure themselves."

His disclaimer as a healer did not prevent him from suggesting that if a woman wished her son to be a painter, during her pregnancy she should visit art galleries and surround herself with beauty and, above all, "think beautiful thoughts." His suggestion echoed the doctrine of acquired characteristics, the belief that we could directly pass along to our progeny the benefits of spending long hours perfecting our skill in bowling or memorizing Shakespearean sonnets. Though this view was discounted by the scientific community, repeating the phrase "Day by day, in every way, I am getting better and better," may have served as a secular mantra to keep parents tranquil during the tempestuous twenties when their daughters were out guzzling bathtub gin and doing the Charleston.

As a result of practicing Coue's method of positive auto-suggestion, I became interested in hypnosis and began reading books on this subject. I wondered whether it was possible for me to hypnotize someone. With more brass than good sense, I asked some friends on the block if they wanted to be hypnotized. At first, they thought I was kidding, but I assured them, with much bravado, that I could hypnotize anyone. Joe Maresca, one of my close friends, challenged my boast.

Following a standard method of hypnotic induction, I asked Joe to close his eyes. I followed this command by suggesting that he was getting sleepier and sleepier. Soon, as my voice droned on and on repeating the same phrase, Joe became deeply relaxed. After some time, I further suggested that he could not open his eyes though I challenged him to try. When he was unable to open his eyes, I was amazed and excited. I could actually hypnotize people.

Encouraged, I proceeded to give Joe a post-hypnotic suggestion. The cue I gave him was that, when I pulled on my left ear lobe, he would begin stamping his right foot. After he was awakened, I waited a few minutes before I pulled on my ear lobe. To everyone's astonishment, including my own, he began stamping his right foot. When I asked him why he was stamping his foot, he answered that it had gone to sleep and he was trying to stimulate it back to normal. At this point, everyone present at the demonstration broke into laughter and applause. I then explained to Joe what had taken place and he joined in the laughter. At that moment, flushed with excitement, I thought to myself, "By God, with this power, I could rule the universe!"

Soon after this demonstration, I wondered whether it was possible for me to hypnotize myself. I decided to try an experiment. One afternoon, I closed the door of my bedroom and lay down on the bed. I induced a state of deep relaxation. When I felt deeply relaxed, I tested myself with these instructions: "You cannot open your eyes…you may try to open your eyes but you can't…you may try to open your eyes but you can't…your eyes are tightly shut…try to open your eyes."

Initially, I thought that giving myself this command was ridiculous. I reasoned to myself, "Of course, I can open my eyes anytime I want!" After prodding myself by repeating, "You may try to open your eyes but your eyes are glued shut!", I decided to show myself just who was in control, the hypnotist or the subject. When I made an attempt to open my eyes, try as I might, I could not. At first, I became annoyed with my inability to even flutter my eyelids. I continued to challenge myself and decided that matters had gone far enough. I made a strenuous attempt to open my eyes but found that I could not. I became anxious and thought, "What if I can't open my eyes? What if I become permanently blind at my age?" Then a foolish grin crossed my face and I thought, "Damn it, it worked!"

At that point, I proceeded to talk myself through the process of becoming de-hypnotized. I suggested to my hypnotized self to relax and at the count of three, my eyes would open. And that is what happened. Needless to say, I was relieved—and exhilarated. But I never tried that experiment again.

When I was inducted into the armed forces, my curiosity about hypnosis had not diminished. I don't know how the Catholic chaplain at the Air Force Base where I was stationed heard about my interest in hypnosis and my offer to hypnotize anyone in the barracks who was willing to volunteer. He called me into his office and condemned me outright as if I were the devil incarnate practicing one of the black arts. I felt that I had been summoned by a member of the Spanish Inquisition and was being judged as a heretic.

During the era of the sixties and seventies, hypnosis and a number of other approaches aimed at healing the human psyche proliferated. One approach that drew my interest was Silva Mind Control. After considerable training, I offered to help my sister-in-law with a minor medical problem. Using positive auto-suggestion and by putting her into a light hypnotic trance, I suggested that her condition would improve. Her husband, my wife's brother, who is a physician, had scheduled a date for her surgery. After one session, her condition cleared up and the surgery was canceled.

When I became a college professor of psychology, my interest in hypnosis was rekindled. What hypnosis has taught me is that mind and body can work both for and against each other. In Mitch Albom's gem of a book, *Tuesdays with Morrie*, I was reminded of this important lesson: I do have some measure of control over how I wish to live my life to the end.

CHAPTER EIGHT

▼

EDUCATION AT HOME AND ABROAD

Education renders a man capable, not only to know and to do, but also...and indeed, chiefly...to be.

John Ciardi

When I was 13 years old, I injured my knee during a baseball game. The dull pain became insistent as I genuflected and knelt serving mass. Our sandlot baseball team could afford a catcher's mask for me, but not shin guards. My injury was diagnosed as Osgood Shalter's disease. The treatment called for a full-length cast on my right leg for the better part of a year. I was forced to miss a year of schooling.

During my long confinement, I read to my heart's content. In my early adolescence, I was drawn to adventure stories, particularly westerns. I devoured more than twenty of Zane Gray's novels; *Riders of the Purple Sage* was my favorite. Gray created cowboys who were three-dimensional, unlike those pictured in the grade B movies I saw. His novels stirred my adolescent imagination so that I pictured myself riding off into the sunset after I had cleaned out the town of bad guys and won the woman of my dreams.

After reading Raphael Sabbatini's novel, *Captain Blood*, I imagined myself a buccaneer. Later, after seeing the movie version of the novel, I fashioned a sword by driving a long stick through a can of Maxwell House coffee to shield blows to my fighting hand. I also gravitated toward books on self-improvement. The Haldeman Julius Company published small paperback books which I could devour in one sitting.

In addition to reading, I occupied myself by making W.W.1 model airplanes. Two of my favorite models were the American Spad and the German Fokker. While convalescing, my cousins would periodically visit me. It did little good to explain to them that the rubber-band models I laboriously put together were not really meant to fly. Each time they came for a visit, they ignored my pleas and crashed my planes into a wall. After they left, I ended up with a damaged aircraft that looked like it had been in a dogfight. It took me the rest of the week to repair the wings and tail.

After making a number of airplanes, I began constructing three-masted sailing ships like the kind I had seen in pirate movies. One challenge was cutting and gluing minute pieces of black thread to create the rope ladders that sailors climbed to tie down the sails. Engrossed in building a model airplane or sailing vessel, I often kept at the task until 3 a.m.

At the end of the year of confinement, the doctor removed the plaster cast that had been autographed by friends who had come to visit. The doctor lifted off the upper portion of the cast, and much to my amazement, I saw my leg covered with long, black hair which came off in rolls to his touch. I tried to convince myself that my hirsute black limb was proof that I was related to dark-complexioned Latin lovers like Rudolph Valentino. I got a big charge when I read H.L. Mencken's description of Valentino as "catnip to women."

I attempted to stay in good physical condition during my year's confinement in a wheel chair by lifting my mother's heavy pots. To exercise my shoulders, I went flying through the rooms of our home at breakneck speeds in my wheelchair.

Instead of being locked in my Catholic education by going to St. Michael's like many of my schoolmates, I went to a non-parochial school. Boys High was located in the Bedford-Stuyvesant section of Brooklyn. During the years before and after the Great Depression, Boys High attracted students from many nationalities—there was no racial or ethnic discrimination. At Boys High, there was rowdiness and roughness but under the control of tough teachers and tougher deans. The school had a reputation for scholarship and had many famous and distinguished alumni who returned to address the student body. The motto of the school is "Noblesse Oblige." The message is clear and direct: You pass on to others what others passed on to you.

To reach Boys High School took an hour by train. I boarded the subway at the 95th Street station located around the block from my home. In four stops, I arrived at 59th Street where I changed for an express train to Pacific Street. I again changed trains to go one stop to DeKalb Avenue, where I crossed over to the other side of the platform to go several more stops to Prospect Park. No longer underground, a shuttle train took me to Franklin Avenue, where I boarded a final train to Nostrand Avenue. All for a nickel! From the train station, there was a ten-block walk to Boys High.

As a freshman, I had the good fortune to have as my history teacher Mr. La Guardia. A man of learning and passion, when he introduced the Renaissance he made the people, places and events come alive. Always animated in his teaching, Mr. La Guardia's fervor rose as he described the Medici family who wielded great power in that phenomenal era. I pictured the storyteller as a nobleman in the royal court of this illustrious family.

Being an ardent Italian-American, as well as a scholar, Mr. La Guardia derided pupils from Italian families who were not diligent in their studies. With a look of feigned disgust, he referred to such sluggards as "pineapples!"

Thinking back to my days at Boys High, I recall another man named La Guardia, who was very different in appearance and style from my history teacher. Fiorello La Guardia, "Hizzoner" Butch La Guardia, also nicknamed "The Little Flower," as mayor of New York City, left an indelible imprint on American political consciousness.

Mayor La Guardia, an incorruptible public servant, had a fierce sense of justice, a hatred of corruption, and a love of fine government. He referred to mobsters as "punks" and "dirty chiselers" and tracked them down like a bull dog.

Undoubtedly this country's most colorful mayor, then and now, La Guardia was easily recognized by his short and stout appearance and his black sombrero-type hat. I remember his high-pitched voice as he read the funnies over the radio during a newspaper strike. Indefatigable, he wielded a baton on Parents' Day in Central Park and wore a fireman's hat and coat to chase down a four-alarm.

In my graduating class at Boys High, twelve of the fifteen students admitted to the Scholastic Hall of Fame were second-generation Jewish-Americans; the other three honors went to two Italian-Americans and one African-American. Dominick Barbiere, Italian-American, was elected to the Scholastic Hall of Fame with a 96-percent average. He was also vice-president of the graduating class. Paul Selice, also Italian-American, was unanimously elected class Kibitzer, had a 93-percent average and was editor-in-chief of *Echi D'Italia*, the school's newspaper.

One of the reasons Jewish-American students garnered most of the scholastic honors at Boys High was the high value that their parents placed on education. Immigrant Jews sensed that the way their children could climb up and over barriers set by an entrenched society was through education.

Italian-American parents telegraphed mixed signals to their children. "Get an education but don't change." "Your first allegiance is to the family; books are okay but learn to use your hands and get a job." To be "ben educati" for immigrant Italians was to have their children value "la via vecchia"—to be devoted to the family but have minimal involvement in American institutions. Unlike many Italian-Americans who gave priority to finding a job after high school, I, as well as a number of my cousins, obtained a college degree.

Richard Gambino, Professor at Queens College where he headed the first Italian-American Studies Program in 1973, reports that there were very few Italian-American college teachers to serve as role models. At the time of his report, he found that only three to six percent of CUNY (City University of New York) faculty was of Italian descent. At the several colleges where I taught, I was one of the few professors who was of Italian heritage.

If Italian-American students didn't excel in the classroom at Boys High School, it was another matter on the playing field. They made a large contribution to the strong athletic teams at Boys High. One oversized star player, a tackle on the football team, sat next to me in music class. When I sang a wrong note, I felt his hand squeeze my shoulder. I was careful not to sing wrong notes at his side.

I joined the gymnastics club at Boys High. But what spurred my interest in developing my physique came about serendipitously. One day, after classes were out and I was on my way to the subway, I stopped at a used magazine and book store. My eye caught the cover of a *Health and Strength* magazine. I was stunned by the physique of the man on the cover. His name was John Grimak, the Arnold Schwarzenegger of his day. I bought the magazine and, on the subway ride home, I read it cover to cover. The next day, I returned to the store and purchased all the remaining *Health and Strengths* in the bins. By good fortune, there was a man in the neighborhood who was moving and was glad to sell me his two-hundred-and-ten-pound set of weights. Within six months, by working out faithfully every day for an hour or more, my biceps swelled from twelve to fifteen inches, and my chest expanded from thirty-six to forty inches.

One hot summer evening, when I came to the dinner table in my undershirt, the family looked at me in amazement. I sent my photo to the *Health and Strength* magazine. It was printed in the Success Story section. Joe Maresca, a schoolmate from St. Patrick's, also became interested in body-building and we worked out together. Soon other friends joined us. I started a body-building club and began instructing weight-lifting to the other boys in the club. Without verbalizing it, I had adopted as my motto, "If you want to learn anything, teach it." Little did I know that I would, one day, make teaching my career.

Body-building went hand in hand with my interest in gymnastics. The members of our club practiced doing headstands and handstands, flips and one-arm planches. We became obsessed with finding challenging surfaces upon which to balance. Besides homemade parallel bars, we did handstands on small stools, park benches and diving boards. To show off, I did handstands on high cement walls, which was not very smart. I became the unofficial instructor of the club. Years later, when I was in the Air Force, my official position was Physical Training and Rehabilitation Instructor. Teaching seemed a natural role for me to take.

Besides lifting weights and doing gymnastic stunts, our body-building club posed for numerous group photos. One stratagem to impress girls was to flatten a newspaper under the upper arm to puff up our biceps. Another ploy was to tense the latissimus dorsi muscles to give the upper body a V shape. I heard comments like, "Boy, I wouldn't want to meet you in a dark alley." It felt great to receive this recognition which bolstered my ego and encouraged me to train harder.

Weight-lifting paid off in a practical way besides bolstering my wobbly self image. During one summer vacation, I worked in a warehouse lifting hundred-pound bags of dried beans. At first, I worked with a man in his late twenties who was built like a bull. For him, lifting the heavy bags of beans required little effort. I knew how strong he was after we wrestled among the bean bags; he was definitely stronger and he never let me, or anyone else in the warehouse, forget it.

Then I was assigned another partner who could barely stand up, much less lift a heavy bag of beans. I soon found out why my new co-worker was not up to the job. One Friday afternoon after we finished work, he invited me to a corner saloon he frequented. He sat at the bar and repeated his order for boilermakers, a lethal concoction—one shot glass of whiskey, followed by a glass of beer. After trying out this combination, I was almost paralyzed. On the train ride home, my head was swimming and it was with some effort that I talked myself into working out with weights when I arrived.

My scholastic record at Boys High was sufficiently respectable to admit me to another tough school, the City College of New York. In thinking back to my four years at Boys High, perhaps I might have done better had I put more energy into my studies and less into physical development. The outcome of my attention to body building is reflected in the caption next to my photo in the *Boys High Senior Recorder*. The caption reads: "Savage (a college noted for its physical training curriculum); Swimming Team; Glee Club; Gymnastics Club; Leaders Corps. HE THINKS HE'S THE SCHOOL TARZAN; HE EATS BRICK ICE CREAM, ROCK CANDY, AND MARBLE CAKE." Though I took pride in being a Boys High graduate, I had not developed a strong identification with the school or with any of the students. Hence, I never attended a class reunion.

Before I met Mr. La Guardia, I felt that having Italian ancestors was nothing to affirm or brag about. In fact, I thought people who came from Anglo-Saxon backgrounds were superior. At St. Patrick's Church, I was under the tutelage of four Irish-American priests. Most of the sisters at St. Patrick's School had Irish or German ancestors. While I don't remember being the butt of criticism from either the priests or sisters because of my parents' heritage, I do remember being shocked, one day, when I met a crone staggering across the sidewalk directly toward me. Drunk, flailing her arms, she screamed, "Get out of my way, you Wop!" That incident remains etched in my memory and alerted me to other demeaning names for Italians like "Dago" and "Guinea." It did not lessen the pain remembering that incident when I learned that "Wop" originated as an acronym applied to Italian immigrants who arrived at Ellis Island "With-out-papers."

Perhaps it was the movies, more than any other source, that distorted my early image of being an Italian-American. Italians in the movies were typecast as clowns, crooners, gigolos and gangsters. When Chico, the "Italian" of the four Marx Brothers, spoke "broken English" like an immigrant from southern Italy and performed antics playing the piano, I rocked with laughter as did everyone else watching the movie. Without being aware of it, I began internalizing the stereotypes which the movies and the media projected and, in doing so, I felt some shame at being of Italian descent.

Only in my later years did I come to appreciate the message of Joseph Alioto, former mayor of San Francisco. "In that great book we call western culture, or the western canon, or the culture of the world," Alioto states, "if we took out the Italian contribution, it would be a pretty thin volume." The Italian legacy he cites is impressive: sculptors like Michelangelo, painters like Da Vinci, musicians like Verdi, poets like Dante Alighieri, navigators like Columbus, scientists like Marconi, military leaders like Garibaldi, political thinkers like Machiavelli, saints like Saint Francis, and, not least, sinners like Casanova.

Italians and opera have always been closely associated, and for good reason. In Italian culture, yesterday's superstar was Caruso; today, it is Pavarotti. Italians and popular music are also closely associated in

American culture; Frank Sinatra and Tony Bennett top the list of world-class singers of popular songs. The movies made in the thirties and forties typecast Italians as gigolos; Caesar Romero was a prototype. Perhaps the most powerful and demeaning image is that of Italians as gangsters, members of the mafia. It is strange that those who portrayed the role of the Italian-American gangsters, as did Edward G. Robinson in *Little Caesar* and Paul Muni in *Scarface*, were Jewish-Americans.

Al Capone, a second-generation Italian-American, became the archetypal gangster during the era of Prohibition, in the decade in which I was born. Ironically, Capone characterized himself as a self-made man and a rugged individualist, not so different from the Henry Fords and Andrew Carnegies, prototypes of the American-American, also men wielding enormous power. Capone claimed that though their methods of operation were different, all three had the same goal: getting ahead. For this reason, he reported in an interview, "Us fellas (meaning Ford and Carnegie and himself) have got to stick together."

Though Capone did not identify himself with an Italian mafia, the image of the "casa nostra," as originating with Italian-Americans, has stuck.

Rudolph Giuliani, former crime buster and now mayor of New York City, points out that all ethnic groups have an equivalent of the mafia. Italians, however, carry the stereotype due to Hollywood publicity and torrid press coverage. Unfortunately, *The Godfather* trilogy, directed by Francis Ford Coppola, and *Goodfellas*, directed by Martin Scorcese (both brilliant second-generation Italian-American film directors), have reinforced this image. Coppola accurately portrayed the saga of some immigrants who took whatever measures were necessary to survive in a country not overly hospitable to newly arrived foreigners. Coppola defended his movie by noting that it could just as well have been the story of the Kennedys or the Rothchilds, a story about a dynasty which demanded personal allegiance to the family.

In more recent years, this myopic image of the Italian-American has begun to change, with pictures like *Marty* and *Moonstruck*, which celebrate rather than demean the character of a people whose contributions to civilization are indeed rich.

A more positive image of Italian-Americans was further reinforced with the advent of World War II. Though Italy sided with Germany, there was no question about the allegiance of Italian-Americans; over five-million were in the armed forces. Several of my cousins became officers.

The day I was drafted, August 4, 1943, Americans were fighting a war on two fronts, the South Pacific and Europe. I was sent from the induction center in New Jersey to Denver for basic training. In prime physical condition, I did not have any difficulty meeting the stiff physical requirements facing new recruits. However, twenty-mile hikes with a full pack made me wish I were back dancing on the smooth floor of a ballroom rather than trudging along the rough surface of back country roads. On one such hike, while we rested briefly, our troop leader, a former commando, noticed the small book I had sticking out of the back pocket of my fatigues. To his query, "Whaddaya reading, soldier?" I replied "*Lord Chesterfield's Letters to His Son.*" He gave me a strange look. I would have been better advised to answer, "*Ten Nights in a French Brothel,* Sir!"

Following basic training, I was sent to Alamogordo, New Mexico. I was disqualified from flying due to an early ear impairment and assigned to Galveston, Texas, as a Physical Training Instructor.

My preference for calisthenics over K.P. was noted in one issue of *The Gulflight,* the Galveston Air Base newspaper. The article reported that Physical Training Instructor and ace weight lifter, Cpl. Frank Calabria, recently performed a 210-pound military press, a 240-pound bench press and a one-arm bent press of 175 pounds (I weighed 155 pounds at the time). The reporter added that, "…while his feats were darn good lifting, you should hear him moan about lifting those nasty trays while on KP duty up at the mess hall."

In another issue of the camp newspaper, when the results of the physical fitness tests were reported, it was noted that the scores of the base personnel had shown a fourteen-percent improvement over the previous test scores. Everyone was pleased about that improvement, especially the members of my department. It was also reported that the highest PFR score on the air base had been made by Cpl. Frank Calabria of Section G, who scored 18 pull-ups, 115 sit-ups, and ran the 300-yard shuttle run in 51 seconds.

I was discharged from the Air Force after a stay of thirty months. I returned to civilian life starved for intellectual stimulation. During that fall, I went to see forty plays, both on- and off-Broadway.

My picture in *Health and Strength* magazine at the age of sixteen started a chain of events I could hardly have anticipated. Soon after my picture was published, I received a cordial letter from a doctor living in Greenwich Village. He wrote how impressed he was by my photo and asked to meet with me. The next week, we did meet at his apartment, which was filled with artifacts from around the world. My admirer was a ship's doctor, an intelligent and cultured man in his forties. He offered me my first taste of a martini and I became hooked on the green olive. After our drinks, he treated me to a Chinese dinner at a nearby restaurant. I was inebriated by the two martinis and gratified to talk to someone who was well-read. I felt grown up.

After our first meeting, he invited me for a return visit. I accepted a number of such invitations, each time anticipating the taste of the martini with the green olive. Our first meeting established the routine: pre-dinner drinks, a visit to the Chinese restaurant and back to his apartment for conversation. This continued until one evening when, having returned from dinner, he showed me several albums of male nudes. I looked at the photos and it suddenly dawned on me why a man who had traveled the world over would take an interest in a boy who had barely been outside of Brooklyn. How naive I was!

A bit shaken by the revelation, I made some nondescript comments as I thumbed through the albums, and came up with an excuse to leave shortly afterwards. We met several more times, even though I had become somewhat uneasy in his company. He never brought out the albums again, nor did he make any overtures to suggest his interest was more than paternal. After an absence of several weeks, he wrote that he had resumed his duties as a ship's doctor. I never saw him again.

I would like to think he enjoyed my company, even though I did not fulfill what I assumed were his needs for a partner who was both a companion and lover. This was to be my first meeting with a homosexual—and it would not be my last. In a subsequent experience seven years later, it was my hunger to share my interests in literature and the arts that brought me to a second encounter which ended as did the first. In both instances, I felt sad that our relationship ended in their disappointment.

My quest for self-improvement included not just developing my body, but also my personality. Dale Carnegie's book, *How To Win Friends and Influence People*, became my bible during my late adolescence. Carnegie, following in the footsteps of the prototypical American go-getter Benjamin Franklin, revealed how to become a successful human being. Through observation and research, Carnegie found that people who smile frequently are viewed as more attractive and are better liked than those who do not. For the next few weeks, I went around smiling like a deranged idiot, and to my amazement, found that what Carnegie said worked.

Carnegie further recommended that remembering names was another sure way to attract people. For the next few months, each time I made a new acquaintance at a social gathering, I focused on repeating the person's name a number of times. To my amazement, the method worked. I became intoxicated with my new-found skills and their effectiveness.

I simulated an interest in whomever I talked to, whether I was interested or not. I was on the way to becoming a clone of Willie Loman in *Death of a Salesman*. I not only wanted to be liked but, like Willie, I wanted to be "well-liked." My attempts during adolescence to become "the perfect specimen," worked for and against me in the years following.

Before I was inducted into the armed forces, I completed my freshman year at the City College of New York. CCNY was founded in 1847 as The Free Academy. It remained tuition-free for one-hundred-and-twenty-nine years, until 1976. Founder Townsend Harris declared the intent of this institution of learning: "Open the doors to all...let the children of the rich and the poor take their seats together and know no distinction save that of industry, good conduct and intellect."

At the opening ceremonies on January 27, 1849, President Horace Webster admitted the first class of 143 boys and said, "The experiment is to be tried, whether the highest education can be given to the masses, whether the children of the whole people, can be educated." CCNY was a gift of the gods to those students who, like myself, wanted to continue their education but whose parents could not afford to send them to a private college or university.

A *New York Times* reporter referred to CCNY during the thirties and early forties as "the Poor Man's Harvard." Albert Einstein, in the twenties, delivered a series of lectures on his theory of relativity at CCNY. In 1995, CCNY was identified as sixth in the nation in the number of graduates who had gone on to earn Ph.D's. It was a tough school. During my freshman year, I barely kept up with my studies and failed math, the only academic course I was ever to fail.

When I was discharged from the service, I was filled with indecision. I knew that I did not want to pursue a career as a physical education teacher, my declared major when I entered college. My on-the-job training period in the service had been instructive; I was not a jock and had little lasting interest in sports. I went through a series of tests and interviews at the Veteran's Administration and here were the results: my computation, mechanical and scientific interests were low; my persuasive, literary, artistic, musical and imaginative interests were high; my social, individual and home adjustment was high; I was emotionally average and economically radical. My advisor felt I would do well as a teacher or a salesman. Ironically, my overall profile was not one well matched to that of a psychologist, the profession I ultimately chose.

I decided to give sales a try. Selling correspondence courses in New York City with its abundant educational resources was like carrying coals to Newcastle. Being a Fuller Brush salesman was not much to my liking—especially after having my foot crunched in a door.

Over the Christmas holidays, I agonized whether to seek other selling jobs or return to school and complete my college education. What helped me make a decision was seeing *Apartment for Peggy*, a movie in which a returning veteran is faced with a similar dilemma. He chooses to return to college even though he has grave doubts as to whether he will succeed, having been out of school for many years.

I re-enrolled at CCNY, this time as a marketing major. Under the shadow of probation, I did well in all my courses, though I was not overly excited about the subject matter. I must have sufficiently masked my negative gut feelings about my choice of a major, for I was elected president of the Marketing Society. The faculty advisor for the society invited a number of his former business associates to address the students in the society. I listened to the presentations of these successful businessmen and noted the favorable responses of my classmates to these lectures. At one meeting, in shock, I realized how little in common I had with those who had made it in the business world and with those who were aspiring to follow in their footsteps.

One course I enjoyed in the marketing curriculum was Industrial Psychology. The professor held a doctoral degree in industrial psychology and had his own consulting firm. As part of the coursework, he required that we assemble a scrapbook, with suitable references, which illustrated the scope and importance of industrial psychology. I got caught up in the assignment and handed in a well-documented seventy-page report. I was surprised to receive an A+++. After class, the professor asked me whether I had considered the field of psychology for a profession. Based on my overall performance in class, he felt that I should give the matter serious thought. That was all I needed to hear. At the end of that semester, I changed my major to psychology. With that move, I propelled myself from a trudging student into a self-generated dynamo.

During the two years I spent at the downtown campus of CCNY, I sought to develop and nourish my interest in the arts and humanities. I filled a notebook with poems, wise sayings and journal observations that I laboriously typed.

Included in my collection of more than fifty poems were, "She Walks in Beauty;" "How Do I Love Thee;" "To His Coy Mistress;" "Go Lovely Rose." You can guess where my head was. In moments of daydreaming, I could imagine myself imitating one my favorite literary characters, Cyrano de Bergerac, winging his words to Roxanne, who stood swooning on the balcony above him.

As to memorable sayings, I collected these nuggets of wisdom which are forever true:

"Know Thyself;"
"Neglect not the gift which is in thee;"
"Neglect not the gift that is in others;"
"The morning hour has gold in its mouth."

Being a morning person, this last wise saying was a reminder to me to make good use of the hours I spent commuting to school.

In my adolescent quest to "understand women" (like Freud, I queried, *"What do women want?"*), I found these quotes to be insightful, if somewhat irreverent:

"The last study of mankind will be man; the last science will be psychology; and its last subject will be women."

"What passes for woman's intuition is often nothing more than man's transparency."

"For every woman who has made a fool out of a man, there has been a woman who has made a man out of a fool."

"God made the earth, then rested; God made man, then rested; God made woman, and since then, nobody's rested."

Leaving for school early in the morning meant being jammed up against other subway riders. Reading a book or newspaper was out of the question. I decided I could hold three-by-five cards close to my chest the way W.C. Fields held his playing cards in a poker game. On these cards I typed excerpts from my notebooks. On other cards, I recorded words that I wanted to add to my vocabulary, so that I might communicate with more precision and even with a dash of color. Some words like *curmudgeon, bravado, canny, flout, virtuosity, hurtle* and *verve,* I saved for special occasions to impress my dates or school friends.

The psychology curriculum at the uptown campus was exemplary. The head of the department was Gardner Murphy, a towering figure in the field, someone who followed in the tradition of America's greatest psychologist, William James. When Professor Murphy came to the end of his model lecture, I felt like I was four feet off the floor as I left the classroom.

Over the next two years, I satisfied all the requirements for a bachelor of sciences degree and was, subsequently, accepted into the prestigious graduate program in clinical school psychology. I was in full stride. At the completion of the graduate program, I was awarded a Clinical

Fellowship. I felt I could successfully deal with whatever obstacles lay before me.

One day my supervisor in the graduate program called me into her office. We exchanged pleasantries and in an off-hand sort of way, she asked me if I had ever been in therapy. I wondered why she asked me that question and, immediately, felt uncomfortable.

"No!" was my immediate and emphatic reply. When she further inquired, in a pleasant-enough tone, if I had ever thought of going into therapy, I felt she had added insult to injury. Immediately, I took a defensive posture and thought to myself, "Why would someone thirty years old, a successful graduate student of psychology, and a Clinical Fellow to boot, need psychotherapy?"

Were it not for the fact that I respected the competence of my supervisor, I would have dismissed her inquiry and passed it off as a routine question asked to all those training to become psychologists. However, when she added that after reading my case reports on children I was testing, she sensed that there might be some "unfinished business" in my life, I sat full upright.

I interpreted her reference to "unfinished business" as a tactful way of saying that, while I was not a full-blown mental case, there probably were skeletons rattling around in my family closet. Not to appear closed-minded, I said that I would give the matter serious thought and thanked her for the names of two therapists she recommended.

The way I went about following the two leads she gave me should have alerted me to my unstable mental state. I set up appointments with both therapists on the same day. Call it compulsivity if you like, but I scheduled one therapist meeting in the morning, and the other in the early afternoon. Sheer masochism!

The morning interview was with a psychiatric social worker who had received her training at the William Alanson School of Psychiatry. She was a middle-aged woman with a fair complexion and light blue eyes. She appeared to be a kind person, and there was even an air of serenity

about her. Despite her appearance and demeanor, from the first questions she asked, I began to unravel and my anxiousness mushroomed
during the remainder of the interview. Though her questions were
straightforward, my answers became more and more muddled and dis-
jointed. At the end of the hour, I felt unglued and could hardly wait to
quit the room. Once outside the door, the only thing I knew for sure was
that I would never return to work with her. That much of a masochist I
was not.

The afternoon interview was with a clinical psychologist. He was also
straightforward in asking me questions. However, I carefully avoided
making any comments which might lead to further questions that
would then raise my anxiety level. I came away from this interview with
the feeling that I had spent a pleasant hour in conversation with a colleague. After I left his office, I felt sure of one thing: I would return to
work with him.

Despite my initial reactions to each meeting, I spent a hellish week
undecided. I was unquestionably rattled by the first therapist I visited. I
rehearsed both exploratory interviews and remembered how my anxiety level had taken a quantum jump with the woman therapist. Sensing
that whatever major conflicts I had were focally related to my mother in
particular and to women in general, I reasoned that choosing a female
therapist might bring my problems more readily out into the open. At
the end of the week, I decided to begin therapy with Clara Rabinowitz.

For the next three years, excluding summer vacations, I met with my
therapist each week for a fifty-minute session. Beyond dealing with the
deep issues related to my mother, other conflict areas were brought to
the surface. Early in our therapy sessions, my resentment toward the
Catholic Church surfaced, resentment for its instilling in me feelings of
guilt and shame related to sex. My spiritual indoctrination had left me
with the belief that becoming physically intimate with a women outside
the bonds of marriage was not only taboo but a sign of degeneracy.

Shortly after beginning therapy, I had a dream which filled me with shame and guilt. I only remember this dream fragment: I defecate on my therapist's chest. At first, I wondered why I had made my therapist the target of this vulgar act, for I had only positive feelings for someone who was trying to help me. Not unfamiliar with psychoanalytic theory, I could recognize my negative transference—the real target of my anger was not my therapist but my mother. Though I sensed my therapist was none too pleased by the imagery of my dream, she did not make me feel guilty or ashamed for my disclosure.

My associations to this dream brought back memories of my mother toilet-training me and how ashamed she made me feel when I soiled myself. That dream also brought back the anger I felt but could not express. In those early months of therapy, I had to come to terms with the "Old Witch" side of my mother.

When I completed my one-year fellowship, I enrolled in the doctoral program at New York University. Those five years at New York University gave me my first taste of the "Old Boys" tradition in the world of academia. Several of the full professors in my department were schooled in the tradition of "Father knows best!" I avoided contact with them as much as I dared. I was respectful though, for they wielded the kind of power which could affect my reaching my academic goal.

Not all members of the graduate faculty were grounded in the "Old Boys" tradition. One of my favorite teachers, Prof. Tietz, did not fit into this archaic academic mold. Understandably, he never rose high in the power structure of the department but he was loved and respected by his students. He always greeted me with a spirited, "And how is the dance master?" His greeting transported me to the time of Louis XIV when the dance master was a person of stature, someone who was the arbitrator of custom and decorum. When Prof. Tietz retired, many students and close friends came to pay him tribute. In the Yiddish language, he was a mensch.

Another teacher to whom I felt drawn was Professor Villemain, who taught courses in Educational Psychology. He attracted a coterie of junior faculty and graduate students who were drawn to the ideas of John Dewey, an American philosopher whose writings have a moral focus. There was an air of idealism, even conspiracy, when we met at the home of the Villemains. Years later, the film *Dead Poets Society* brought back memories of this inspiring teacher.

In the throes of completing my dissertation, I took a much-needed break and signed up for an inexpensive student tour to Europe. In France, I anticipated going to locales that had spicy reputations. In Spain, I would meet friends of my classic guitar teacher who would take me places to hear authentic flamenco music. In Italy, I looked forward to being in a culture whose influence on my early life was profound.

Americans embarking on a trip to Europe is a familiar theme in literature. In taking my first trip abroad, I felt like I was taking the time-honored journey of the hero. This image of the hero in search of adventure might have been better reinforced had I embarked on a three-masted sailing ship like Captain Blood, my movie hero. Instead, I was booked on a small Dutch steamer that was far less glamorous. While my accommodations left much to be desired, they were, no doubt, better than the living arrangements my mother had to endure when she sailed to America. However, I did have a small taste of what it must have been like for her as our ship wobbled and tossed on the high seas.

What I hadn't anticipated in signing up for this particular tour was that my fellow passengers would be undergraduate students all younger than me, some by as much as ten years. My shipmates were enrolled in Ivy League schools and were spoiled brats. Throughout the trip, they plagued our guides by insisting that their every whim be met. Our age differences, however, did work in my favor. When we met each of our tour guides, I found that I had much more in common with them than with my shipmates. The close relationship I formed with all four guides proved a highlight of the trip.

In France, I fell in love with our guide, Jacqueline Pouissant, and even doubled back after the full tour to see her again. Slim in build, her delicately turned nose and dark eyes captivated me, as did her movements which resembled those of a little bird. Though she was forced to live frugally, the way she arranged her scarf over her simple dress announced a woman of refined taste. Jacqueline had the sensibilities of an artist and though she did not paint or sculpt, she responded to the works of artists in a way which would have pleased their creators.

On one occasion when I accompanied Jacqueline to the Louvre, she stood in front of one painting fully absorbed for what seemed forever. Her description of the painting made the artwork come alive for me. Her sense of appreciation applied to whatever she encountered, whether it be a Charlie Chaplin film, or the architecture of Notre Dame Cathedral. From her perspective, it was a more rewarding experience to fully appreciate one art object than to give cursory attention to many. Though it was difficult for me to devote that kind of attention and concentration on our tour, which included visiting three European countries in the space of two months, I will never forget the lesson she taught me.

In contrast to the rich life she lived in the realm of the arts, her everyday life was poor in material means. I visited her in her small, one-room apartment with its antiquated bathroom situated in the hall. Jacqueline's mother had died when she was young; she saw her sister and father infrequently. The money she earned as a tour guide barely paid for schooling and books.

On our last meeting, she wore a new dress with a different scarf; her ensemble probably cost her a month's rent. At our parting, in the Luxembourg Gardens, I kissed her on the cheek and gave her an expensive art book that I knew she would prize but could ill afford. Though I sensed that she had a strong liking for me, I felt she was a loner and valued solitude more than a close relationship with a man. Her parting words, that I was a good person, an ambassador to bridge her culture and my own, made me feel inches taller.

If my meetings with Jacqueline made my heart beat faster, going to the Naturisti, a nightclub in the Place Pigale, titillated more primitive senses. I learned from Francis, our male guide, that the Follies Bergere was a tourist trap but that the Naturisti was an authentic showcase for the senses: beautiful women, elaborate costumes, romantic music, exciting dancing and ribald humor. In one brief skit, a spotlight shone on the soles of two pairs of upturned shoes; after a momentary blackout, one pair of feet changed position from pointing up to pointing down. After each act, Francis would voice his delight by saying, "C'est extraordinaire!" I returned to see the show a second time and could not help comparing the Naturisti with Minsky's Burlesque House, in Newark, New Jersey—as a young man out to sample forbidden pleasures, I saw at this burlesque house a bunch of oversized women with big breasts who went through their bumps and grinds mechanically, as if they were pornographic puppets.

If France gave me my first flavor of Europe, it was Spain that made me feel I was on familiar territory. My classical guitar teacher, who had been born in Cuba, had made frequent trips to Spain. He gave me the names and addresses of several of his friends; in addition, should I be interested, there was a brothel he recommended.

I looked up Marcelo Barbero at his guitar shop on the outskirts of Madrid. He gave me a cordial welcome when he heard who had sent me. Small in height and gentle in demeanor, he said he had a medium-priced guitar that would please me. What misadventures I had with that guitar will soon be described. Señor Barbero was to be my contact to meet John Perrin, an American expatriate, who had gone to Spain to study the flamenco guitar and was still there after seven years. The day after I arrived in Spain, and before our tour began, Marcelo directed our taxi to Perrin's quarters. What followed for the rest of that marathon day reads like a chapter out of James Joyce's Ulysses.

Juan Perrin, the Spanish name he went by, lived in an unkempt one-room apartment. Not yet out of bed, he apologized for his disheveled appearance; his pajamas were punctuated with holes. Juan explained that he was waiting to move into luxurious quarters soon. I later learned that he depended upon a monthly allowance from his grandmother in the states. The day he received the check, he would spend it in a grand manner, and then mooch off his friends for the rest of the month. Outside of being a braggart, Juan was a likable person. The one day I spent with him was, unquestionably, one of the highlights of my trip to Europe.

With Juan as my guide, we began the day with a breakfast of black coffee and rolls at a tasca. Juan insisted on paying for the breakfast. It was the last time he paid for anything for the rest of the day as we made the rounds of cafés, bars and other places he frequented. The owner of one clothing store where Juan bought his shirts gave us a warm welcome, offered us an aperitif and invited us to to the back room to play on his flamenco guitar. Walking along the boulevard, we met a tall, gaunt flamenco singer. His appearance reminded me of Don Quixote. Looking forlorn, he said he was doing penance for the shabby way he had treated his wife after coming home drunk after an all-night binge with his friends.

We then proceeded to a small café, El Cuchio. Juan introduced me to Mario Escudero, a famous flamenco guitarist, who was practicing in a small room below the bar. Juan left me with Mario and went off to do some business. An hour later, he returned with another flamenco guitarist, Pepe Montes, and the show began. Mario and Pepe were a study in contrasts. Mario was tall and slim, his classical Spanish features those one might see in a painting by Valesquez. Pepe was short and bulky; his face and physique those Goya would paint. These strong physical contrasts were reflected in the way each played the guitar.

Even before Mario finished practicing one of his pieces, Pepe, seemingly in a rage, yanked the guitar out of Mario's hands. He then commenced playing a soulful solerares mimicking the lyrical style with which Mario had played this piece of music. The look of disgust on his face projected the feeling: "You call that playing?" He then proceeded to play a lightning-fast alegrias with its upbeat feeling. It almost seemed that he would rip the strings off the face of the guitar in his rendition of the music.

When Pepe finished his solo, Mario regarded him with an amused smile, a smile mixed with benign contempt. Wresting the guitar out of Pepe's hands, Mario proceeded to play in the flamboyant style of his contentious friend to let him know that he could match his histrionic performance. Once he had demonstrated that he could duplicate Pepe's style, Mario resumed playing as he had before the contest began. Back and forth the rivalry continued: challenge was met with response.

Juan whispered to me in the midst of this spirited exchange that what I was witnessing was an event which had never occurred before. What he said may well have been true, though it is not unlikely that he set up the whole performance for my benefit so that I would keep paying for the drinks which kept arriving. Whatever his intent, Juan did afford me an opportunity to hear, at close range, two superb flamenco guitarists. In the journal I kept during my trip to Europe, I recorded that meeting as a peak experience.

Later that afternoon, we met Marcelo who treated us to lunch at a famous restaurant where suckling pig was a specialty. The small bar we had just come from had had olive pits strewn in the sawdust on the floor. This restaurant had colorful paintings of bullfights and flamenco dancers on the stark white walls. The suckling pig was a treat and Señor Barbero insisted on paying the bill.

This leisurely lunch was followed by more meetings with Juan's friends as the afternoon slowly gave way to evening. When I asked Juan where it would be possible to hear a flamenco singer accompanied by a guitarist, he went about setting up a fiesta. We entered a building with a nondescript exterior. Inside was a series of rooms occupied by groups of men who were drinking and conversing. Juan made preliminary arrangements to hire a guitarist and singer for a fiesta, but his plan soon got out-of-hand as his friends dropped by to be treated to drinks. I must give my host credit for pulling me out of a situation which would have cost me more money than I was prepared to spend. Despite being disappointed that no fiesta could be arranged, that day would be one I would never forget.

I paid Señor Barbero for the guitar. However, since my tour was leaving the next day and I did not want to burden myself with carrying it for the rest of the trip, I left the guitar with Juan. He promised he would ship it to my home in the states. Of course, he never did. A year later, it was my brother-in-law, studying medicine in Madrid, who was finally able to trace the guitar to a pawn shop. I never heard from Juan again, and were I to try and locate him, no doubt, I would have to look under every table, in every bar, in Madrid.

While I was in Madrid, I had another memorable adventure of a very different kind. Taking the lead given me by my guitar teacher, I went to the brothel he recommended. Why? I was curious. I had never been to one. Paul Tournier said this about the human urge to travel: "The real meaning of travel, like that of a conversation by the fireside, is the discovery of oneself in the dialogue." Going to my first brothel, there was very little conversation and commitment in the dialogue, but I did discover that underneath the studious exterior of a graduate student was a "dirty young man."

When I entered the brothel, the challenge was how to go about selecting a bed partner and what to do afterwards. Before I had time to reflect on these two questions, I was greeted by two matronly women dressed in black, who came to settle on the price. They assured me that their establishment was visited by dignitaries and high government officials who always went away satisfied. After the price equivalent of ten American dollars was agreed upon, five women in various stages of undress paraded before me. I chose the one who looked most Spanish to me. Would you believe her name turned out to be Carmen?

She led me to a room which seemed out of a picture book on the decline and fall of the Roman Empire. On the walls were murals of lovers in intimate embraces. Two white columns stood as sentinels to a sunken bathroom replete with a bidet and a large bathtub framed by mirrors. In these surroundings, I began to feel decadent even before I disrobed.

A second surprise came when Carmen slipped out of her clothes. I could never have guessed that she was so well endowed. From the start, I took an active role to prove to Carmen that I was an accomplished lover by putting into practice all that I had learned from an Arabian treatise on love. I was tempted to believe that she enjoyed our long encounter, for she continued her dalliance. After this episode, I noted in my journal: *I've had it. I have paid for my first and last woman.* Famous last words!

The next day I went back to the brothel and to Carmen. There were other houses I visited in different cities of Spain. After each visit, I faithfully recorded in my journal: *That's it!* But I was becoming a brothel addict. Not that my later experiences improved upon those that had gone before. In fact, they got progressively worse. There were houses that operated as if they were street-corner markets, with milling crowds of men examining a parade of women. And in this melee, older women, always dressed in black, shrilled as they bargained with customers and attempted to clear the entrance rooms for more potential customers.

Our guide in Spain was German-born Walter Klaus, who spoke Spanish fluently and knew the city and countryside intimately. I soon learned that his intimate knowledge of the terrain extended to other intimate knowledge. At the end of a day's tour of museums and churches, Walter instructed me at a corner taverna on the fine points of coaxing a woman from bar to bedroom. He also shared the address of a brothel he favored. I followed through on this lead and had a disagreeable encounter with a woman who was very attractive but emotionally volatile. This visit ended my exploration of the world of brothels.

Before leaving Spain, I went to a nightclub which featured professional flamenco dancers, musicians and singers. The performance was polished and I was filled with admiration. But, I could hardly contain my excitement when I visited the Gypsy Caves in Granada. Here were gypsies, born and bred, who performed with less polish than those professionals I had seen at La Zambra, but they danced with more spontaneity and genuine feeling. Seated in the center of a room with whitewashed walls decorated with religious icons, was a matriarchal figure, her legs wide apart, her two feet planted firmly on the floor. She cast a critical eye on each dancer's performance. Accompanying the dancers were three flamenco guitarists and two singers. The combination of dancers, singers, and musicians created the spirit of a true fiesta. My joy knew no bounds.

When we arrived in Italy, I felt most at home. I knew enough Italian to communicate directly with the people I met. The food I ate reminded me of my mother's cooking. It was easy to see where the animated gesturing my relatives used in communicating originated. Italians, it is well known, talk with their hands. I know I do. And among born and bred Italians, as well as among Italian-Americans, there is more than a hint of the ham actor. It was natural to see, in the streets of Italy, men hugging other men, and even walking with each other arm in arm. Fortunately, I grew up hugging members of my family, male and female; I kept to a handshake when I encountered someone with an Anglo-Saxon background.

Our guide in Italy was Bindo Modigliani, a young man in his late twenties. He reminded me of my father as he appeared in a photo taken when he was Bindo's age. Small in stature, soft-spoken and gentle in manner, Bindo loved his country, its arts, music and natural beauty. He deepened my sense of all three worlds and filled me with pride for my Italian heritage.

We toured Rome, Florence and Venice, visiting the places highlighted in every guide book. I was amazed at how different and unique each city was. I now understood why Rome was known for its elegance, Florence for its art, and Venice for its romance. I particularly enjoyed Florence, a museum without walls. Because my father was a sculptor who venerated Michelangelo, I was particularly interested in seeing the works of this extraordinary artist. Next to the commanding figure of David and the panoramic paintings in the Sistine Chapel, what stirred me most were Michaelangelo's later sculptures in which his figures seem to be emerging live from the stone. What daring!

Grand opera, as the world knows, is synonymous with Italian opera. Yesterday it was Caruso; today it is Pavarotti. What could be grander than hearing Verdi's *Aida* performed in the Baths of Caracalla, an open-air theater cradled between the hills of the countryside? I went to see the Palio, in Siena, a horserace like no other—the track has square corners. I was caught up in the pageantry of men in ancient attire waving colorful banners, each banner representing a social club which had sponsored a horse in the race. For a small country, everything appeared to be larger than life in Italy.

Sitting outdoors at a café in the piazza was like being in a "Theater in the Round." Compared to their cousins in the north, Italians in the south like to cut "la bella figura." My uncle Pep once told me this story about what happened when he returned to his hometown after being in America for a number of years: The town major, wanting to impress my uncle during their walk in the piazza, said to him, "You see the man who is coming toward us? He will have to salute me." As he predicted, when they drew near, there was a courteous exchange of greetings, but it was clear who was "top man."

Though our student tour took place during the summer vacation rather than in the spring when the Italian countryside is at its loveliest, the gardens of La Villa D'Este, in Tivoli, and the Blue Grotto, in Naples, were resplendent with beauty, as were the fountains at Navona and Trevi. I understand why Byron, along with legions of other writers, rhapsodized Italy. Their reactions: "See Italy and die!"

While returning to the United States on the slow boat that had taken us over, there was time enough to reflect upon my first journey to a foreign land. With my experiences in Italy fresh in my mind, I really began to understood the sense pride my high school teacher, Mr. La Guardia, felt for his Italian heritage.

Ten years after being discharged from the armed forces, I completed my graduate studies. I had survived a decade crammed with schedules, classes, appointments and examinations. When the chairman of my dissertation committee came out of the room after deliberating with two other members of the faculty for what seemed an eternity, he was grinning. A shiver ran through my body when he held out his hand and addressed me as "Dr. Calabria."

With the completion of my academic training, one door closed and other doors were about to open. During that eventful decade, I had taken some wrong turns and, for a time, lost my direction. If someone was looking out for me, he or she finally put me back on the right path.

CHAPTER NINE

▼

DANCING: MY PASSION

I am sure to include dancing in my life, because spontaneity connects me to my soul.

Angeles Arrien

My earliest recollection of dancing is painful. I was not yet fourteen when I went with my parents to visit my cousin Vinny. To me, every-thing about my cousin was larger than life. He was seven years older, tall, handsome and a sharp dresser. Vinny was enrolled at Savage College and was majoring in physical education. He also taught at an Arthur Murray Dance Studio. On the afternoon of our visit, Vinny and his partner, Shirley, also a dance teacher at Murray's, performed a rumba and tango which brought much applause from all members of our assembled families.

While everyone gathered around Vinny and Shirley to congratulate them, I was jealous and sulked in a corner of the room. I was wearing a hand-me-down suit, a vestige of the days of the Great Depression. I tried to draw attention to myself by stringing a watch chain across the pockets on either side of my vest. While I hoped the watch chain would be noticed, inwardly, I felt ridiculous.

I was sixteen when I went to my first dance. I thought it time to become a man, a ladies' man. I would gain this status by cutting a dashing figure on the dance floor. My model was Rudolph Valentino. In *The Four Horsemen of the Apocalypse*, the swarthy gaucho bends the pale-faced heroine to his will as he leads her in a torrid tango. According to newspaper accounts I read later, Valentino's sensual gyrations in this film caused women in the audience to swoon. A captive of my adolescent fantasy, I dreamed of arousing my dance partners to such heights of abandonment.

The opportunity to test my mettle as a ladies' man was at hand. A few days before my first dance, I asked my older sister to show me a few basic steps and how to hold a girl. Armed with this rudimentary knowledge of ballroom dancing, I went with high expectations to the Friday evening dance social at St. Patrick's School.

As I entered the school building, I tried to assume Valentino's macho air, but immediately felt like a jerk. Besides, the ambiance at the church social was much different from that in a cabaret. In place of the semi-dark room where Valentino gyrated to the slow, pulsating music of the Argentine tango played by a band of gypsies, the school auditorium was brightly lit, the walls of the large room unadorned, and the music came from a phonograph.

Besides, Valentino did not have to reckon with Father Reardon patrolling the auditorium dance hall to make sure there was no more than eight inches of space between partners. He was in agreement with that Irish curmudgeon, George Bernard Shaw, who quipped that dancing is "a perpendicular expression of a horizontal desire." In his welcoming speech to the girls and boys at the dance, our spiritual mentor cautioned us to be wary of what awaits us in the next world should we indulge our carnal desires either by action or fantasy. This religious homily was sufficient to dampen my adolescent ardor.

My first dance, the occasion to leave a memorable imprint on my soul, turned into an experience I would just as soon forget. The dance began promptly at eight o'clock. As I entered the auditorium, I tried not to appear anxious as I made a quick survey of the girls standing and seated on the other side of the hall. I assumed a cool demeanor as if I were Cary Grant.

I began this silent dialogue with myself. One part of me said:

"Well, it's time to ask a girl to dance. That girl with the long brown hair and nice figure looks good."

The other part of me replied:

"Naw, it's too early to start right in. Wait until the next number."

When the next record was played, my adventurous side was ready to give it a try, but my cautious side invented another excuse not to get started. This fruitless exchange continued until intermission. Sad to say, when the dancing resumed, so did my 'infernal' dialogue. As the evening drew to a close, my craven side had complete supremacy and got in a parting shot: "It's too late to ask anyone now; I guess I'll have to wait until next week."

The next week and for weeks afterward, I went through the same dumb dialogue at each dance. Of course, the real reason I was unable to ask a girl to dance was my fear of rejection. My cautious side had no problem scaring me with thoughts of what would happen when I crossed to other side of the dance floor, where the girls were bunched together, and asked a girl to dance. She would look me over and flatly turn me down. What a fool I would feel like. To torture myself further, I fantasized that the other girls nearby would naturally assume there was something wrong with me, like having bad breath.

Many years later when I saw the film *Marty*, I had a sense of déjà vu'. Marty, like myself a second-generation Italian-American, went to a dance and the first girl he asked turned him down. I felt a knot in my stomach as if it were happening to me.

A month went by before I worked up the courage to ask my first girl to dance. She had brown hair, a nice figure and looked Irish. I was not aware that she was preparing to leave the dance. In declining my invitation she was pleasant enough, but I was crushed. The next week I worked up courage to ask another girl to dance. When she accepted, I was encouraged to keep trying. But I found that I was not always successful. It might have helped had I known that even Joe Di Maggio, my baseball idol, didn't get a hit every time at bat, and he was "The Great Di Maggio."

It might also have helped to know that, when my father first came to America, he was also shy when it came to dancing. At family gatherings, my aunts and uncles would tease him until, at one party, to everyone's amazement, he got to his feet and danced the latest steps of the Charleston he had learned at a dance studio. His nimble performance earned him the nickname "The Kimble Kid!"

By my late teens I had long since lost my shyness at dances, for I frequented the St. Patrick's socials. When I was inducted into the armed forces, little did I know that this call to serve my country would transform me into an avid ballroom dancer, and, additionally, launch a part-time career as a ballroom dance teacher.

That opportunity opened when I was assigned to the Galveston Army Air Base as a Physical Training and Rehabilitation Instructor. On weekends, I took the bus to the Galveston United Service Organization. Ms. Shearson, a woman in her early forties with a mature figure and a warm disposition, was in charge of the entertainment program. It felt good to be greeted by my surrogate mother when I walked through the door of the canteen, my home away from home.

I associate the U.S.O. with big band music. At home and overseas, G.I.s listened to Glenn Miller and Tommy Dorsey. It was on one flight overseas that Major Glenn Miller lost his life. Though he did not visit Galveston before his tragic death, his records were always played on the juke box; his arrangements were copied by the live bands who played at the U.S.O. One arrangement in particular, *In the Mood*, made every dancer on the floor come alive. If I had a good dance partner, when the band played the final, rousing chorus, I would go into a Dionysian frenzy.

After several months of attending the Saturday evening dances at the U. S.O., I approached Ms. Shearson with the idea of my teaching a dance class before the evening social. Understanding my enthusiasm for dancing, Ms. Shearson granted me permission to begin a dance class. What she didn't know, and what I somehow neglected to mention, is that I had never before taught such a class. With more chutzpah than real knowledge, I gave my first dance class. I was gratified when I received a sound round of applause at the end of the class. Skills I learned working as a physical training instructor, like how to break down complex motor movements into simpler components, were of help. Instructing these classes gave me my first real taste of the joys of teaching.

In addition to receiving many compliments for the way I conducted the classes, I forged new friendships, especially with women. Once again, I tested the maxim and found it to be true: "If you want to learn anything, teach it!"

It was at these dances at the U.S.O. that I became keenly aware of the differences in women's bodies. Holding a partner close, it would be hard not to notice that some women had breasts that were soft and spongy, while others had breasts that were firm and pointy. Another observation: to lead effectively, I found that I had to be in firm contact with my partner. Some of my partners were comfortable with my lead; others were not.

Dancing with a girl who had long legs and a short torso was difficult. When I found a partner who had a perfect fit for my body and who could dance, there was the sheer delight of body flight. Some of the women I danced with could have modeled for a beauty pageant, but they were stiff and ungraceful. Conversely, some women who were graceful dancers were trapped in ungraceful bodies.

There were a few women I met at the U.S.O. who seemed to have it all, figure and rhythm. One such paragon of beauty was Rose Marie. Whether it was the cleavage she revealed as she bent forward over a pool table, or the way she undulated doing a torrid rumba, Rose Marie had a winning combination

After I was discharged from the service, I obtained a license from the New York State Board of Education to teach dancing in their Continuing Education Programs. That experience opened up more opportunities than I could have imagined.

Teaching dancing was a labor of love. I was paid $6.50 an hour for a four-hour class. One school where I taught was located in Coney Island, an area heavily populated by first- and second-generation Jewish-Americans. It was not unusual to have well over a hundred students in a class, with ages ranging from thirty-five to seventy-five years.

The small income I received from these classes was supplemented, later, by giving private lessons in the basement of my parents' home and teaching groups at social organizations, country clubs and private homes.

Teaching small groups at private homes was more profitable, and it had perks. After the dance class, our hostess would invite the class for refreshments. It was on these occasions that I developed a taste for steamed clams, lox, cream cheese and bagels.

Though Brooklyn was alive with dance clubs, it was New York City that was the Mecca in the 40s and 50s, the "Golden Age of Ballroom Dancing." Two of my favorite places in the heart of Manhattan were Roseland and the Palladium. At Roseland, billed as "The Home of Fine Dancing," you could dance to both an American and a Latin band. If, however, you wanted to dance exclusively to Latin rhythms that sizzled, the Palladium, "The Home of the Mambo," was the place to be.

At Roseland, on Tuesday nights, at one end of the large dance floor, the best dancers in the five boroughs of New York congregated. If there had been a Social Dance Hall of Fame, John Luccese and Jo Nobles, and Vic Wilson and Rose Girard would have headed the list. On Thursday evenings, those who were preparing to enter the Harvest Moon Ball practiced their dance routines. On Sunday afternoons, there was a mix.

One evening, on my way to the subway after leaving Roseland, I was tempted to see what it was like inside one of the "Dime-a-Dance" halls, located on Broadway. In addition to blown-up photos of overly made-up, blonde hostesses, "Dime-a-Dance" showcases displayed enticing advertisements such as: "50 Beautiful Lonely Hearts To Dance With YOU!"; "75 Glamorous HOSTESSES Waiting For You!"; and "Dance In ECSTASY with 100 Gorgeous Beauties!"

"Dime-A-Dance" halls cater to older salesmen, out-of-towners, loners, servicemen and ballroom-lizards. Out of sheer curiosity, I decided to explore what I imagined were "dens of iniquity." Sheepishly, I moved toward the entrance guarded by a doorman dressed as a Cossack. He handed me a "Special Cut-Rate Tonight Only" card. I climbed a steep flight of stairs, paid the small price of admission and received a ticket which read: "One Free Dance." Once inside the dimly lit dance hall, I was assailed by the pleading voices of a dozen harpies: "Dance, Handsome?"; "Take me!"; "Please dance with me, Sweetheart!"

Immediately, I was flooded with a multitude of sensations: embarrass-ment, excitement, hesitancy, bashfulness, uncertainty and amusement. To cover my confusion, I assumed the posture of a cultural anthropologist doing field research—in this instance, my subject was taxi dance halls where you get taken for a ride. Fearful that if I chose any particular partner, the other women would tear me limb from limb, so I gave myself over to the hostess nearest me. She led me to the small dance floor and when I put my arms around her to begin dancing, I felt her clammy bare back and smelled her cloying perfume. We danced for exactly one minute before a buzzer rang. It was the signal to hand over my free dance ticket.

After the free dance, Bunny, my dance partner, directed me to the ticket booth to get a string of ten tickets for a dollar. It was then that I remembered the name of a song I associate with the Great Depression, "Ten Cents A Dance." Bunny led me back to the small floor where we commenced to dance. It seemed we had hardly begun to move around when the music abruptly stopped. I automatically tore off a ticket and handed it to Bunny.

Soon, I began to feel like an automaton: dance one minute, hand over a ticket, dance another minute, hand over another ticket. Once I got over being frustrated by the stop-and-go dancing, I began to relax and enjoy what seemed a scene out of a Fellini movie. Ten tickets was all I needed to see how the system worked.

Years later, I was delighted to read Leo Rosten's description of his experiences at several taxi dance halls. In his book, *People I Have Loved, Known or Admired*, in the chapter entitled 'Dime-a-Dance,' Rosten brought back the flavor and ambiance of my experience in the dance-hall demimonde.

One Tuesday night at Roseland, a nondescript-looking, middle-aged man with wire-framed glasses approached me as I left the dance floor. He introduced himself as Mr. Sachs and commended me on my dancing. He next inquired whether I would be interested in meeting a dance teacher who was looking for a professional partner. He added that there would be engagements at prestigious Manhattan nightclubs such as the Chateau Madrid and the Havana Madrid. Flattered by his offer, I agreed to explore his proposition. My fantasy took reins when he left to fetch her. I anticipated meeting someone who looked and danced like Ginger Rogers.

When he returned, my dream dissolved as I saw my prospective partner—a blonde, middle-aged woman who wore too much makeup. It was also not difficult to tell that she had had plastic surgery on her nose. Our meeting was cordial and Donna smiled pleasantly when I told her I was completing my graduate training in psychology. She may have felt it was a bonus finding someone who could not only dance, but could speak the English language without mangling it like a stereotypical Brooklyn Dodgers fan.

Nor did her dancing ability make up for her lackluster appearance. Donna was not a "natural" as a dancer. Despite my initial disappointment, I did accept her offer and was in for some pleasant surprises. To put some flash into our mambo routine, she hired "Killer Joe," the effervescent emcee at the Palladium Ballroom. He choreographed and taught us a routine in preparation for our engagement at the Chateau Madrid.

Among Latin dances, the mambo is a dancer's dance; performed well, it is a show-stopper; performed poorly, it is an object of derision. After some practice at Donna's small apartment where she gave private lessons, we were able to perform a mambo routine which was credible, but hardly a show-stopper.

Opening night, I was costumed as a rumba dancer in dark trousers and a white shirt with ruffled sleeves. I danced my mambo routine with Donna and received polite applause from the guests, largely friends of Mr. Sacks and Donna. As part of the routine, I performed a "tornillo," a stunt which required going into a deep-knee bend on one leg. I arched my body back so that my upper and lower body were parallel to the floor. Donna held me in this position with her right hand, then proceeded to twirl me around and around if she were stirring a batch of cake mix. In the midst of performing the "tornillo," I felt a snap in my knee. With some effort and not a little pain, I was barely able to resume an upright position and continue dancing. Fortunately, I had only pulled a muscle, an injury which healed in a few days.

At another performance, this time at the Chateau Madrid, I blanked out while performing a choreographed waltz routine. I faked the routine by repeating the same step over and over again, much to my partner's displeasure. I soon learned that to perform a dance routine skillfully required much time and hard work. Being a professional dancer was not all glamour.

What puzzled me was how Donna, given her mediocre caliber of dancing—my own skills were better, but hardly professional—could be invited to perform at these prestigious Latin nightclubs. That mystery cleared up when I found out that Mr. Sacks, besides being one of Donna's ardent admirers, was a high-ranking member of the Masonic Order where he called upon influential friends.

With the coming of summer and without college classes to attend, I agreed to become Donna's partner at the Nevele Country Club, a popular year-round resort in the Catskill Mountains of upstate New York. Once again, Mr. Sacks used his influence to gain us entry into a venue where we would, otherwise, not have been invited.

At the outset, Donna modestly identified herself as "Queen of the Dance." To add to this celebrity charade, she introduced me as Frank Castle. Had ballroom dancing had a hall of fame during the 20s, Vernon and Irene Castle would have been easily inducted; this couple was venerated by the media as if royalty. The Castles originated *The Castle Walk,* which captured the fancy of the Charleston generation. Needless to say, I hardly took my stage name seriously and could imagine the sardonic grin such posturing brought to Terpsichore, the muse of the dance.

As the resident dance team, in addition to giving a free group lesson every day, we earned our income from private lessons. The income from these lessons was split fifty-fifty, despite the fact that I taught ninety-percent of the lessons. It did not take long for word to get around that Donna was not an exemplary teacher and, furthermore, she had a short temper. Though I still lacked formal training as a ballroom teacher, I did well enough instructing pupils in the fundamentals.

As a teacher, I had the temperament of an extrovert and the patience of an introvert. It also helped when I was identified as a graduate student well on his way to a doctoral degree. Most of my pupils, all Jewish-Americans, prized education and respected those who went into the professions, particularly medicine. While I was not training to be a medical doctor, valued at the top of the vocational ladder by Jewish-Americans, becoming a psychologist was not considered chopped liver.

I felt fortunate to have a means of earning an income during the summer months when my private lessons dwindled. Despite the unfair division of labor, being a dance instructor at the Nevele brought other benefits. Whatever was available to guests at this classy summer resort was also available to me. Unlike other members of the staff, I ate with the guests and relished the bountiful and delicious food for which resorts like the Nevele are justly famous. Jews and Italians share at least one common characteristic—the love of good food and plenty of it.

Besides the cornucopia of food served at meals, the Nevele had a first-rate house band which played dance music every night of the week. To satisfy the appetite of Latin music lovers, Noro Morales and his band played on weekends. Señor Morales, classically trained, played boleros that sounded as though they had been composed by Chopin.

Besides giving daily lessons, our major responsibility as dance teachers was to stage a Champagne Hour Dance Contest every Friday evening. Hotel guests signed up to compete in these contests. If a contestant had taken private lessons, I would prepare them to showcase a dance. The winning male and female dancer was each awarded a bottle of champagne.

To open the Champagne Hour Contest, Donna and I performed one or more production numbers, usually an up-tempo mambo or a fast-paced peabody. Following these exhibitions, I would dance with the female contestants and Donna with the male contestants. Judging was by applause, so it helped a contestant if they had family and friends in the audience.

One stifling Friday evening, I was so absorbed in making a clay model of one of my father's sculptures, a female nude, that I lost all sense of time. A hurried knock on the door and loud shouts reminded me that, in a few moments, the Champagne Hour was about to begin. I quickly changed from my drenched shorts into a tuxedo.

Decades after my stint at the Nevele, I saw the film *Dirty Dancing*. In the film, Johnny, a dance teacher at a resort not unlike the Nevele, instructs a starry-eyed girl on the dance floor and elsewhere. The movie sensationalizes what goes on at after-hour parties, when the staff and younger guests engage in orgiastic dancing.

Jackie Horner, who worked for Tony and Lucille in charge of the dance concession at Grossingers, the largest of the Catskill summer resorts, recalls that there did exist "Bungalow Bunnies" and "Johnnys" as portrayed in the film. But she also notes that during the 40s and 50s, this scenario of teacher and pupil was more the exception than the rule. In *It Happened in the Catskills*, the ever youthful and vivacious Horner reports that the 50s was more a time of innocence than license. My experiences at the Nevele tend to bear out Horner's observation.

I do not want to give the impression that during my two summers at the Nevele I had taken a vow of celibacy. Being a dance instructor at the Nevele did offer opportunities for sexual dalliance. It was not unusual for women, single and married, to come to the Nevele to have a weekend fling.

During my first summer at the Nevele, I met Norma, who must have come to the hotel with just such an intention. At our first dance lesson, she let me know, by gesture and eye contact, that she wanted more from me than dance lessons. I knew that she was married because her husband visited on the first weekend of her extended stay. It was easy to see why she wanted to seduce me, for her husband was a bore who hardly paid attention to her during his visit. Whatever initial scruples I had in becoming involved with a married woman, my attitude changed when I observed the dead relationship between husband and wife.

Norma was an attractive woman; she had a pleasing mature figure with notable breasts. While I instructed her in dancing during the day, she tutored me in love-making at night. I was a willing pupil. It was the incorrigible Mae West who said that goodness had nothing to do with her many sexual encounters with men. Nor did goodness have anything to do with my relationship with Norma.

When the summer ended, Norma wrote to me. Her letters always had a hint of eroticism. During the fall of that year, Norma came to New York and stayed at a hotel in Manhattan for a weekend. We met in her hotel room on Friday after dinner, and there we stayed. But on Saturday morning, I am ashamed to relate what happened. Instead of remaining in the steamy atmosphere of the hotel room with Norma, I chose to attend a scheduled class at New York University given by the dullest teacher in the psychology department. I rationalized to myself that if I missed his class, I might jeopardize my chances later, should I have the need for a recommendation.

I can imagine what Zorba, my literary mentor, would have said about making that masochistic choice. "Sad, Boss. Very sad!" Zorba would chide me. "You disappoint me, Boss. Here you have the chance to be in heaven with a desirable woman and you choose to listen to a dried-up stick of a man reading out of a book. What kind of a man are you? Sad, Boss. Very sad!"

Later, after the affair ended, I had to acknowledge that Zorba was right. Not everything worth learning came out of the pages of books. Thinking back on this episode, it would appear that while I had rid myself of the sexual straight-jacket of the Catholic dogma of purity, in its place I had donned the hair shirt of the Protestant work ethic.

During my second summer at the Nevele, I met Iris, an unattached, attractive Harvard graduate, whose parents were conservative German Jews. What began as a week-long relationship at the Nevele spilled over to Cambridge and Harvard Square where Iris shared an apartment with another woman. Unlike my relationship with Norma, I became deeply attached to Iris to the point of asking her to marry me. True, she was not a good dancer, but it was always interesting being with her.

One Saturday evening, after I arrived from my five-and-half-hour drive from Brooklyn to Cambridge Square, Iris and I parked in what I thought was a deserted woods. Feeling secure in the dark enclosure of the car, we began frolicking in the back seat. Not long into our fun, two officers peered in the open window, their flashlights shining all over us. Frightened, I scrambled to pull on my pants while Iris seemed to dally as she rearranged her clothing. Her dalliance, no doubt, allowed the officers a generous view of her hips and thighs.

For the moment, I did not understand why Iris acted so brazenly but later discovered she knew exactly what she was doing. The officers, visibly aroused by her free display, gave us only a warning never to come back again. As we drove away, Iris told me, impishly, that this whole episode had happened to her before. Intuitively, in both events, she had adopted the strategy of the stripper; "Give the customers what they want." I wondered in what course at Harvard she had garnered such learning.

On my long return trip to Brooklyn, I mused about this run-in with the police, an encounter which had left me visibly shaken. I tortured myself with the question: *What would have happened if the officers had brought me to the station house and booked me for sexual misconduct and indecent exposure?* This information, entered in my criminal file, might have blemished my character and jeopardized my future career.

To torture myself further, I imagined calling my mother to come to the station house to bail me out. As a young boy, she had been my support and had confronted the nuns at St. Patrick's School when they sent me to the coal bin. In this latter incident, I was a grown man, accused of wanton sexuality in the back seat of my automobile. While my mother would have posted the necessary bail, I would have been reminded, more than once, that if I had not strayed from the Catholic Church, none of this would have happened. Mea culpa!

In retrospect, I am glad that Iris refused my offer of marriage. The more I learned about her, the more it was clear that, like myself, she had personal problems to work out. A meeting with her father and mother, both stern parents, pointed to part of her problem. Iris also told me about her bouts with epilepsy which further damaged her self image.

My love life became further complicated when I realized that Donna wanted me to be more than her dancing partner. She became jealous over any interest I showed in other women. While I was grateful to her for introducing me to the life of the professional dance instructor, I never entertained the idea that she was anything more than a professional dance partner.

After a second summer at the Nevele, Donna and I went our separate ways. I never heard from her again and I did not attempt to contact her. My best guess is that she continued to teach middle-aged bachelors at her Manhattan apartment until Mr. Sacks finally got a divorce and they married.

Donna was my first and only professional dance partner. Soon after we parted company, I met a professional dance couple, teachers who were the genuine article. This meeting came about after I found out about the Saturday evening socials at the Byrnes and Swanson Dance Studio, on Flatbush Avenue in Brooklyn. When I entered the studio, I felt that I was in the inner sanctum of ballroom dancing. On the dance floor were many of the "sharpies" I had seen dancing at Roseland and the Palladium.

I introduced myself to Don Byrnes and Alice Swanson, the owners of one of the most prestigious ballroom dance studios in New York. From our first meeting, I was drawn to Don and Swanee. I immediately recognized that they were true and dedicated professionals in a field overrun by amateurs. Upon hearing my background and experiences, I was invited to join their training class for ballroom teachers. What an eye-opening experience that turned out to be! Having struggled with the challenge of how to most effectively teach both modern and Latin dances, I could only marvel at the clarity with which these two master teachers presented the material.

While the other pupils in the class responded to the classes without visible excitement, I kept groaning under my breath, in unabashed appreciation, "It can't be that simple!" Once, during the course of instruction, when Brooklyn was blanketed by a blizzard which made driving virtually impossible, I was the only one who showed up for class.

What impressed me most about Don and Swanee was the respect they had for the art and science of ballroom dancing, both as teachers and performers. Later, I learned of the outstanding contribution Don had made when he was assigned to Special Services during W.W.II. He organized entertainment for the G.I.s fighting in the Far East and was awarded the Medal of Freedom, the highest honor given a civilian by the United States Government.

After the war, Don and Swanee met with a half-dozen independent studio owners, competitors like John Phillips, to analyze the Latin dances which became popular during the 40s. To insure teaching the rumba and bolero with authentic style, this group of teachers invited native dancers from Cuba to perform. In addition, talented Latin-American dancers from the Palladium demonstrated the mambo and the cha cha. Don and Swanee would then pass along their knowledge at national conventions of ballroom teachers.

After the training classes, Don invited me to join their studio. I felt honored. My contribution when we discussed the dance syllabi was to introduce the vocabulary which I had learned in my college courses in educational psychology. The minute I interjected a concept like "gestalt" and "reinforcement," Don's eyes would light up and he would immediately jot down the term in his notebook. When Don and Swanee published their book, *A Textbook of Cuban Cha Cha and Mambo,* my article titled "Why We Dance" was included in their publication. It was through their influence that I was invited to be on the faculty of two prestigious dance organizations, the Dance Educators of America and the Dance Masters of America.

In gratitude for their generous assistance in helping me improve my skills in teaching ballroom dancing, I wrote a letter of recommendation which accompanied the scrapbooks they donated to the Lincoln Center for the Performing Arts Dance Library. One excerpt from this letter follows:

"Teaching for Don Byrnes and Alice Swanson is nothing less than a vocation. Acknowledging the integrity of each dance, they strive to teach and perform each dance with accuracy and with authentic expression. Even more commendable is their ready willingness to share the fruits of their research with other teachers in the interest of furthering the profession of ballroom dancing."

I left the studio when I received a full-time teaching position at a college in upstate New York. Albany was a far cry from New York City when it came to ballroom dancing. Over the next fifteen years, folk dancing filled the gap. Going folk dancing each Friday evening helped to keep my wife Angela and me on an even keel. Not infrequently, I had to coax her to go dancing after she had had a demanding week raising our four children. Though reluctant to make the effort, once on the dance floor, she became a whirling dervish.

My favorite dances were from Greece, Yugoslavia, Rumania, Bulgaria and Israel. It was not long after my introduction to the abundance and variety of dances from around the world that I started teaching classes in folk dancing.

We traveled to workshops taught by native teachers who could model the authentic style and feeling—the attitude—in performing the dances of their countries. The line of least resistance was to dance all the dances as if they originated in one country. I had to modify the stylized, erect posture of the ballroom dancer in order to simulate the carriage of a sheep-herder doing his dance on a mountain terrain. Speaking of erect posture, at one workshop, a Yugoslavian dance teacher with a limited English vocabulary urged us to "March on with erection!"

We participated in week-long programs at folk dance camps during summer vacations. Our favorite camp, located in Maine, was run by Mary and Michael Herman. Each day of the week, a particular culture became the focus of attention. During one visit, on a brisk morning, my wife and I were pleasantly awakened by the voices of a group of singers dressed in Scandinavian costumes. They served us hot chocolate as we stood barefooted, in our pajamas, on the deck of our cabin. This ritual seemed a more civilized way of being awakened than by the blare of an alarm clock.

We also attended classes given by non-native instructors who had made a special study of the dances of a particular region. One such teacher, Dick Crum, both scholar and dancer par excellence, endeared himself to his pupils and to our family. When Dick stayed at our home during a weekend workshop, he supplied us with an endless source of entertainment. Each time he began double-talking like Sid Caesar, I would end up pounding the floor with laughter. Dick turned out a flaw-less performance of the mangled English of an Italian immigrant and the melodious tonality of a cultured immigrant from India.

Unforgettable was his demonstration to our young children of how to move a rubber band, wrapped around the middle of his nose and around the back of the head, down over his nose, then to his mouth and chin, and finally, to his neck. All this without the use of his hands. Performing this challenging feat, Dick's expression simulated that of a chimpanzee in a Tarzan movie. His performance brought gales of laughter from our children, who all wanted to imitate his act.

For a number of years, Dick choreographed and taught Balkan dances to the Tamburitzans, a highly skilled group of students on folk dance scholarships at Duquesne University. This unique program, which combined academic and performance studies, was initially open to students whose immigrant parents came from the Balkan countries. Before being accepted, each student had to show promise in three areas of the performing arts: singing, dancing and playing a musical instrument. An inspiring thought! What if there were as many college scholarships available to students for their musical talent as there are scholarships for football players?

Our intense involvement with folk dancing afforded us pleasure not only at home, but when we traveled abroad. In Greece, at the seaside resort town of Naflios, my wife and I asked our waiter if he knew of a place, not a tourist trap, where we could see authentic Greek dancing. Dimitri took us to the Sirena Taverna. In the showcase outside the tavern entrance was a photo of our guide dancing alongside several men. As we entered the door, we heard a bouzouki trio playing live music in an enclosure off the small dance floor.

Dimitri settled us at a table and sent over a bottle of resina with his compliments. He joined his friends on the dance floor and what a delight to watch them! After several dances, he invited us to join him. We linked arms and danced the slow hassapiko, my favorite Greek dance. We bent forward, dipped and swayed. I was ecstatic. For the remainder of the evening, we traded steps back and forth.

In Turkey, we found an unpretentious-looking restaurant jammed with people. Once inside the building, we could sense that we were in for an unusual evening.We were seated at a table without benefit of a table cloth and almost immediately we were served a bucket containing several long bottles of beer. Periodically, a waiter would leave a dish of appetizers to accompany the beer; the last offering was a dish of fruit. Everyone was served the same fare.

A four-piece band accompanied two female vocalists; a male singer doubled as emcee. The scintillating music inspired the belly dancer to mount a small table where she performed her sinuous movements. Crowded onto the small dance floor sunken below the level of the tables were couples in a state of frenzy. To add to the excitement of the music, waiters approached the tables with strings of balloons which were purchased, then popped, with lighted cigarettes by the revelers.

When the band began playing a lambada, a gyrating dance that enjoyed a brief popularity in the states, Angela headed for the dance floor. She knew that my last attempt to perform this dance had resulted in an appointment with my chiropractor for a 'lambatomy'.

Not long after Angela joined the dancers, a father left his young daughter and began dancing with my wife. As he hooked on to her waist, he was soon joined by scores of dancers who proceeded to follow the leader as Angela lead a serpentine line around the restaurant tables.

Later, when we abandoned the crowded dance floor, we were invited to join other couples dancing around the tables adjoining our own. At the end of the dance, several men shook my hand, and one enthusiastic dancer gave me a full embrace. Another man had left a cigarette next to my plate while I was dancing. In both Greece and Turkey, we were no longer strangers in strange lands.

When we returned from our trip abroad, I was forced to abandon folk dancing. The bouncing, leaping and bending, part of Yugoslavian, Bulgarian and Greek dancing, began to take a toll on my back and knees. I returned to my first love, ballroom dancing. Angela and I had some catching up to do, especially in converting to the International Style in dancing the foxtrot, the waltz and quick step. Among the several instructors we have engaged as our teachers, none stand higher in our esteem than Jean and Bill Keehan. Master teachers, they continue to inspire us with their expertise and enthusiasm. We feel, indeed, fortunate to be their pupils.

The year I reached the three-quarter-century mark, I had a peak experience that will stay in my memory. The Malt River Restaurant in Albany was jammed with young men and women from Puerto Rico, Cuba and other Latin-American countries. Angela and I began dancing to a sizzling mambo and, not long into the dance, I felt a tap on my shoulder and heard a voice say, "Keep dancing!" Never drawn to dance competitions, I hesitated for a moment whether to continue, but decided to keep on dancing.

One by one, dancers were asked to leave the floor until there was only one other couple left. After ten minutes of strenuous dancing, I felt fatigued and thought I ought to stop. I lead my partner to the sidelines as we watched our sole competitors continue. This Latin-American team, half our age, was recognized for their subdued but skillful style of dancing.

We cheered them along with the rest of the crowd. When the music ended, I assumed the contest had ended, with the winners on the dance floor. Not so. We were invited back for a final dance-off. With encouragement from the crowd, I used every eye-catching move I could remember from my days when I did dance exhibitions. With every new move we performed, the crowd became more and more animated.

The music stopped and our competitors were given a sound round of applause. When the emcee held his hand over our heads, the response we received was amazing. I thought I would lose my hearing, for the sound was deafening. The grand prize was a dinner for two. Of course, the next day, being part bionic man—I have had a back fusion and both hips replaced, not to mention being plagued with chronic arthritis—I was back to see Dr. Weck, my chiropractor, who knew how to put me back together again. My body needed attention after the contest; my soul felt just fine!

CHAPTER TEN

▼

MARRIAGE AND FAMILY:
A COMPLETE EDUCATION

Marriage is not merely sharing the fettucini, but sharing the burden of finding the fettucini restaurant in the first place.

Calvin Trillin

"Mom, I've found the girl we've been looking for!" This grand announcement was the first public declaration to the world that I was smitten by the woman I had recently met at the Byrnes and Swanson Dance Studio. When my mother met Angela, she agreed that we had, indeed, found the girl "we" had been looking for.

As to the beginning of our romance, one Saturday night at the dance social where I was one of the hosts for the evening, Angela arrived with her sister Maruja and her sister's boyfriend. Was it only a coincidence that Maruja, fifteen minutes before leaving for this dance, thought to invite Angela along? Was it fate that Angela, despite all the excuses she could make up, was finally convinced when her sister prodded her with the rejoinder, "What are you waiting for, the Blue Prince to come to your doorstep?" To me, our meeting was pure synchronicity, a meeting written in the stars.

Angela's face, classic Spanish (she is Ecuadorian), her figure, classic Playboy, captivated me. I immediately asked her to dance and to my great delight found that, in addition to being physically attractive, she was a born dancer. Though usually conscientious about fulfilling my duties as dance host, that evening I kept coming back to ask Angela for many, if not most, of the dances.

My frequent return trips did not escape the attention of her sister who, aware of the reputation of dance teachers as gigolos, proceeded to question her about my attentiveness. Maruja was more than a little skeptical when she heard my story: that I was a graduate student about to complete my doctoral studies in psychology; that I was single and had recently broken up with my girlfriend; that I had recently returned from a trip abroad. Protective of her younger sister, she sent her boyfriend to the owner to verify that what I had told Angela was true. "Yes, it is all true," Don reported, and added, to boot, "He is a person of good character." Don's recommendation gave me a green light and when I asked Angela for a date the following week, she accepted. If it was not love at first sight for her, there was a certain chemistry at work which later proved alchemical.

The Saturday after we met, and for every Saturday until we married, I called for Angela at her home in Manhattan. After a leisurely lunch at a small café, we would go to a Broadway matinee, or spend the afternoon at the Metropolitan Museum or the Museum of Modern Art. Following dinner, we danced at Roseland; still later, we went to Birdland to listen to Count Basie or to the Carnegie Recital Hall where Brother Theodore recounted bizarre tales. I timed our arrival to her apartment for shortly before midnight to insure that, like Cinderella, she would not disappear, leaving me only her dance shoe with which to find her again.

My salt-and-pepper mustache and my dark hair, streaked with more than a few gray hairs, initially made Angela think I was too old for her. On one of our dates, she chanced to see a miniature size copy of my discharge papers that I carried in my wallet. She was surprised to discover that we were only four years apart in age. With this discovery, she shifted me from the category of "interesting date" to "potential husband."

Despite this discovery, Angela still had doubts as to whether I was her "Blue Prince." She was puzzled that I would invite her to so many shows in one day, and yet not call her during the week. She also wondered why I did not send her a Valentine's Day card.

What puzzled Angela further was my formal behavior during our early courtship. Whether it was fear of being rejected, or because I sensed that this relationship was precious, I was careful not to offend her by any forward behavior. Holding hands and a brief good-night kiss were the only displays of the ardor I showed her. After we were engaged, I was less reserved.

There is an explanation for my cautious behavior during the early days of our courtship. I tried to minimize distractions. A girlfriend whose character was that of an angel and whose body was that of a siren was unquestionably a distraction. Hence, on that one chosen day of the week, I sought to make up for what may have appeared to be only a passing interest in our relationship.

Our nine-month courtship followed the Italian and Latin tradition of reciprocal visits between the two families. One evening, while Angela was visiting me (I lived with my parents until I got married), a blinding snowstorm ensued. Out of concern, my mother suggested that she sleep over. Her mother, however, insisted that I bring her daughter home rather than have her return the following morning. I did.

During our engagement, Angela remembers the time I sprained my ankle and was bedridden for a week. On the hot summer afternoon she visited me, I was bare-chested when she entered my bedroom. She exclaimed, "Could this be all mine?" To this day, I am not sure whether it was brawn or brains that won her over. My conceit is that it was both.

I proposed to Angela one Saturday night in the month of June. Though I don't remember what I did and said, I would like to imagine I approached her as a knight would his fair lady. Whatever did happen, Angela asked if she could have time to think over my proposal. The next day when we met, she inquired whether I had slept well. In an offhand manner, I said I had. Her rejoinder was, "Well, I couldn't sleep at all." I waited, holding my breath for what she would say next. "Yes," she said. "Yes," she would accept my proposal. I was overcome with joy and vividly recall how the sun streaming in the large windows of the living room of her apartment suffused me with inner and outer warmth.

I should tell you a bit about Angela's background. She was born in Ecuador in 1928 and came to America with her family when she was eighteen. In Ecuador, both her father and mother were trained as teachers and they schooled Angela and her older sister and younger brother, at home, up to the 5th grade. The children completed the remaining years at a private Catholic elementary school before going on to high school.

Because teaching was a low-paid profession in Ecuador, her parents chose to start a business. They purchased one bus, then a second, then others, and soon the family prospered. Angela's mother had a shrewd business sense; her father was a handyman and could fix anything on wheels with a stick of gum and a piece of string. From her mother, she inherited the ability to keep our books straight—without her, I would have ended up in the poorhouse. From her father, she inherited the ability to hear when our automobile is malfunctioning. While her mother was serious, her father was playful. To "toughen up" his three children, he would hook them and himself to a car battery, and they would all join hands in a circle. Mild voltage would circulate through the circle which they formed.

It was Angela's mother, raised as an orphan, who decided to move to the United States so that her children would have opportunities she never had. Her mother also wanted a better marital fate for her daughters than they would receive in a society where married men frequently had lovers on the side. A strong-willed woman, she put her plan into effect, despite the reluctance of her husband to leave the country and their business.

They arrived in America in the late forties. The income they expected from the properties they owned in Ecuador was not forthcoming due to monetary exchange restrictions. With the exception of Angela's brother, who was still in high school, everyone in the family found a job. Angela and her sister worked as artists in a silk-screen business; at night, they attended classes in English at the Latin-American Institute and took courses at Hunter College. Later, with the support of the family, her brother was able to go to Spain and became a physician.

I met Angela ten years after her arrival in America. During that decade, only in one relationship did she consider marriage. Her prior fiancé was also a second-generation Italian-American who had a very close relationship with his mother, a bond not uncommon among immigrant Italian families. In this case, his mother undermined the relationship; marriage plans seesawed and had a negative effect on Angela.

Aware that her daughter's health was strongly affected by indecisiveness, Angela's mother suggested a trip to Ecuador for a vacation. Her mother returned to the U.S. after a short stay, but Angela remained among family members and friends for the better part of a year. During that time, she regained her sense of balance and only decided to return to the United States when her mother faked ill health. When she returned home, her engagement was over. Her prolonged stay in Ecuador had brought an end to the romance.

In contrast to the smother-loving relationship between her former suitor and his mother, my relationship with my mother was, at times, contentious. When this attitude surfaced, Angela wondered if I would respond to her in this argumentative fashion after we were married. What she had not appreciated was that if you are in a wrestling match with an Amazonian contender like my mother, you had better have good moves, else you risked being easily pinned to the kitchen floor.

We set about planning the wedding and hit our first obstacle. When I approached Father Smith, still serving as parish priest at St. Patrick's Church, he took a stern attitude at my having left the church. We explored other arrangements and met no resistance at the Catholic church Angela sometimes attended.

We married on September 23, 1956, my thirty-second birthday. I chose this date as insurance that I would never forget our anniversary and thereby avoid the resulting marital grief. In retrospect, I don't think it was such a brilliant idea since I am no longer the center of attention on my birthday.

Our wedding followed tradition; after the church ceremony came the reception. My mother was the natural choice to be in charge of the wedding reception, for she had prior experience with my two sisters' weddings. Her banquet choices had a measure of class: the food was delicious, the drinks plentiful, and the music exhilarating. When it came time to dance the introductory waltz, *Let Me Call You Sweetheart*, unlike couples new to ballroom dancing, Angela and I danced gracefully together. It was a good augury for our marriage.

During the wedding celebration I was completely relaxed. I remember feeling genuine warmth and affection for everyone at the wedding. Had I been a king on that day, I would have generously parceled off lands to deserving nobles. Had I been a governor, I would have pardoned criminals from execution. Had I been Don Corleone, I would have, at least for that day, heard the petitions of family members and friends and granted their wishes.

Throughout the ceremony and afterwards, Angela was radiant. It was after midnight when we retired to our hotel room. Being frugal, our accommodations on our wedding night left something to be desired. Still, after we showered, we listened to some of our favorite music on tape. We drank champagne and consumed the night in the passion and love we felt for each other.

The next day we left for Europe on a six-week honeymoon. Our first stop was London. For a week, we toured and saw Kew Gardens, the Tate Gallery, and a Flamenco show in which the premier dancer, Antonio, performed with his sister. We then went to Spain for a week, and spent the remaining time in Italy, where we drove from Milano to Palermo.

Unrealistically, we planned to stop at Santa Sophia to pay my mother's sister and her family a brief visit (an afternoon or so). I should have known better, given the Italians' sense of hospitality, and the fact that I was the first one from my family to visit our relatives in Italy. We stayed four days.

Our arrival in the village seemed staged as though on a Fellini set. We turned off a main artery onto a dirt road barely indicated on the map and came to the village square. At first, there was no one in sight. Then, all at once, as if a film director had given the signal, scores of men, women and children poured out onto the piazza. Soon, our Fiat was surrounded by a crowd of people. My fourteen-year-old cousin presented my wife with a bouquet of roses. There was much hugging and kissing at every turn. Then began a formal ritual of welcome.

A short, rotund man wearing a black fedora, black baggy trousers and vest, a white shirt with red garters on the sleeves and a black tie addressed us: "Youa me, wea glad yu ahere." He then added several more sentences in broken English. I mustered my best Italian and returned his greeting. When he heard me respond in his native tongue he seemed flustered as if I were speaking an alien language. Then, without missing a beat, he repeated his original speech beginning with: "Youa me, wea glad yu ahere." I later learned that our greeter had lived twenty years in Chicago and had learned as many words. By greeting us in this manner he had made a "bella figura." I could understand why he was taking such a prime opportunity to show off the benefits gained from living in America.

With what seemed half the neighborhood crowded into my aunt's house, out came the food—special cakes and breads that had been baked that morning, wine and other Italian goodies—and out came the guitar and mandolin. From the time we arrived until the day we left, it was a party. We were treated as royalty and the humble dwelling we stayed in was better than a room at the Jolly Motel (Italy's version of the Super 8). Each night, Angela and I sank exhausted into our down mattress, almost disappearing from each other's sight.

Before we continued on our journey, we took my aunt and two of her children on a trip to La Sila, a nearby mountain resort. What amazed me is that, despite her proximity to these mountains, my aunt had never made this trip. I thought to myself how different my mother's experience was compared to her sister's. My mother had traveled three-thousand miles to America, while her sister had not even ventured as far as this mountain. My mother had gone to New Jersey, Cincinnati and Chicago, and had made side trips to Florida. Compared to her sister, my mother was a world traveler.

When we left my mother's family, an incident occurred which made my wife have second thoughts about the man she had married. On our way to Sicily, we paused on the road to rest when an old man approached us and asked for food. Always ready to give to someone in need, Angela reached into a bag of taralas, a parting gift from my aunt. Before she could open it, I grabbed her arm and admonished her not to give the man any of the biscuits. Her look was one of astonishment and I could intuit the question forming in her mind: Had she married a miser, a Silas Marner, someone who would deny a piece of bread to an old man in need? I reached into my pocket and gave the man money. The explanation for my behavior followed, although I am not sure it fully satisfied my bride.

What I sought to make clear to my sweetheart was that one of my fondest memories related to eating was waking in the morning and having a tarala to dip into my breakfast coffee. Taralas are like Italian bagels. They are made of dough, first boiled in water, then baked so they have a firm golden crust but are soft inside. What gives a tarala its unique flavor are the anise seeds embedded in the dough. If my mother made a large batch and they lasted for over a week, the taralas would harden. Eating one without first dunking it could result in a broken tooth. Of course, there was always a nut cracker or a hammer to do the job if you did not want to chance a trip to the dentist. To this day, if any of my nieces want to curry the favor of their uncle, they will make me a batch of taralas. My behavior related to this food of my childhood has not changed. With my bag of taralas neatly stashed away, I am forever vigilant, watchful that no one discovers my hiding place.

Our extended stay in Santa Sofia meant that our plans to spend several days in Sicily had to be abandoned in order to catch a flight back to Rome. It was more than a fair exchange. In place of visiting ruins from the past, we had visited my relatives very much alive in the present.

I was gratified to hear my mother being praised by her family and friends for her beauty and goodness. But I could also detect a trace of self-sacrifice and martyrdom in my mother's sister, similar to the attitude my mother took to instill guilt, an attitude that drove me to anger.

Had we followed the dictates of our heads instead of the urges of our hearts, we would not have planned such an extended honeymoon. To finance the trip, we had to combine our savings with money we borrowed. We reasoned that once we were settled with jobs and perhaps bambinos, we would not be able to easily satisfy our interest in travel. Within two years of our honeymoon trip, we had paid all our debts.

When we returned to the states in early November, we moved in with my parents. The prospect of me immediately finding a position as a psychologist seemed slim. As it turned out, within two weeks I found a position as a research assistant on a project that was winding down after five years of research. The focus of the research was teacher effectiveness. When this project terminated, my supervisor, having found a new post in upstate New York, alerted me to a one-year opening at the State College at Albany. Though it meant moving away from family and friends, we agreed that taking this appointment was a good way to launch my teaching career.

Our first home was a one-bedroom apartment in a housing project in Albany. We lived there for three years. Our living room by day became our bedroom by night with the help of a Castro convertible sofa. The birth of our first two children further stretched the limits of our small space. While our available space was diminished, our life experiences greatly expanded when we became parents.

Trying hard to convince ourselves that small is beautiful, we purchased our first car, a VW Bug. On our periodic weekend trips to visit our families in Brooklyn and Long Island, it was a feat of engineering to fit two adults, two children and luggage into our shoebox-size vehicle. Strangely, our children have fond memories of being in the "toaster," the small space behind the back seat, intended for luggage but a perfect place for two small bodies.

Our first son, Carl, was born a beautiful child. Our second son, Mark, on the other hand, was born with a shock of black hair, sideburns to rival Elvis Presley and a shadow of a mustache. When Angela's sister came to visit at the hospital, she said in jest, "Este se te dano." ("You ruined this one.") Soon, all that hair faded away and Mark turned out to be a very fine swan indeed.

I knew from my studies in child psychology, as well as from common knowledge, that our sons would be different. When our older son awakened early in the morning, it was sufficient to call his attention to the jungle gym strung from either side of his crib, and while his bottle was being heated, he quietly entertained himself by spinning the rattles and beads overhead. When his proud parents awakened him to show off to family and friends, he was all smiles and sociable and it was not difficult to put him back to sleep.

With our younger son, it was another matter. No way would he be distracted while his bottle was warming up. Only when the bottle was securely settled in his mouth would his cries subside. When his proud parents awakened him to show off to family and friends, it was impossible to put him back to sleep. We quickly learned to not even try.

At the end of my one-year appointment, I went back to being a researcher, this time for the State Education Department in Albany. In addition to my day job, I taught courses in the Evening Division of Russell Sage College. At the end of two years, I accepted a position in the Psychology Department of Russell Sage College in Troy, New York. After one year at Sage, and feeling sufficiently secure at that post, we decided to buy our first house.

Our new house in Albany had four small bedrooms and was in a neighborhood which housed many families with young children. Alissa, our first daughter, was born at this new home. While we had not planned to have four children, another daughter, Mayela, was born two and a half years later. Accidents do happen and she was a most welcome addition, after all.

Observing the quality time our grown children now devote to their own children, I wish I had devoted more attention to them when they were growing up. Not that I was a negligent father. Alissa remembers me reading her Dr. Suess's *The Cat in the Hat* and *Green Eggs and Ham*. Since I had virtually committed these books to memory having read them countless times, to this day, when I am in a mindless mood I go about repeating to myself excerpts from *Green Eggs and Ham*. So far, no one has stopped me on the street as I mutter to myself, "Sam, could you eat them in a tree, in a field, in a boat, in a house, etc., etc., etc. ?"

When I received an appointment in the Psychology Department at Union College in Schenectady, we began looking for a larger home, one near the college. Our search took more than a year, but we were finally rewarded with a home that was beyond our wildest dreams. When our diligent real estate agent described this house as having eight bedrooms, I wondered whether we would have to have more offspring to fill up all the spaces.

At first glance, the aluminum-sided house was not impressive. However, as soon as we walked through the carved entrance door with its oval, beveled glass, and into the foyer with its ornate staircase, then into the kitchen with two staircases, one alongside the other, our interest grew. And when we entered the spacious living room, separated from the beamed-ceiling formal dining room by great oak sliding doors, Angela and I exchanged knowing glances. The fact that there was another prospective buyer for this house waiting outside the door pushed us to a quick decision. For no more than today's price of a quality automobile we purchased this house in the now historic General Electric Realty Plot.

In 1662, Schenectady had been purchased from the Indians. Two years earlier, there had been a massacre in the Dutch trading settlement in which 70 inhabitants were killed and 30 taken captive. Schenectady was chartered as a city in 1798. The Erie Canal was opened in 1825 and along with the Mohawk and Hudson Railroad, the area prospered. Today, Schenectady, like other old American cities, is struggling to attract newcomers to the area.

Thomas A. Edison moved his Edison Machine Works to Schenectady from New York. It later became the corporate giant, the General Electric Company. By 1890, Schenectady's population exploded to 20,000, by 1900 to 32,000, by 1910 to 73,000, and by 1920 to 89,000. This influx of new employees gave Schenectady an urban landscape, as large tracts of land were parceled off and homes built on them.

Our home, originally owned by Percival Lewin and located in the General Electric Realty Plot, was built in 1908. It is listed in the National Register of Historic Places. Dr. Bruce Maston, a local physician, imaginatively conceived a publication he titled *Enclave of Elegance,* which describes many of the homes in the G.E. Plot. The day they photographed our home, my mother was visiting us with Ginger, her neurotic dog. The photographer captured my mother seated on our porch, knitting, with Ginger sitting alongside her anxiously peering around as if waiting for an extraterrestrial object to land on her head.

Next to the Percival Lewin house was the home of Charles P. Steinmetz, the technical genius and colleague of Thomas Edison. Unfortunately, his home was demolished 22 years after his death; the city could not afford the upkeep. They did, however, name the location Steinmetz Park, and erected a small monument to his memory. Doing some archeological digging in the park when they were young, our two sons unearthed test tubes and small bottles from Steinmetz's home and laboratory.

Bordering Steinmetz Park is a small, wooded area with a stream that runs down through the Union College grounds a block away. Walking to work through the wooded area along the the stream, I felt refreshed when I arrived for my morning classes.

As parents, the wheel of fortune turned in our favor and landed on the number four. That lucky number reminds me of a visit our family paid to friends from our folk dance group. Over a period of ten years, Bill and his wife, Jean, had been building a fifty-foot tri-maran, a sailboat with three hulls, in their backyard. We wanted our children to see their colossal creation. The day we chose to visit happened to be misty; a slight drizzle had begun as we approached the backyard gate. Perhaps, as we entered, it was the overcast day and the sight of my bearded friend who looked like a Biblical prophet that gave me the eerie feeling of being somewhere else in time. I felt the spirit move me whereby I hollered to Bill, who was working on top of one of the massive hulls, "Noah, we've brought two of each kind!"

Naming one's children is one way of acknowledging that each is unique. The fact that our children are so different from one another should not have surprised a professor who taught classes in child psychology. The text I used in class noted that within the first five weeks of birth, a whole range of individual differences are manifest to the discerning eye. The response of our two sons to the morning bottle has already been cited. Not so surprising, these personality differences continued throughout the years.

Take, for example, our sons' eating habits and preferences. Eating for Carl was, more or less, a necessity for living, while for Mark, a joy—his face beamed as he twirled his fork around strands of spaghetti. It did not surprise us that, after he married, Mark designed his home around the kitchen, which is outfitted to satisfy the exacting needs of a chef working in a four-star restaurant.

Both sons have professional careers, Carl in computer design, and Mark in mechanical engineering. Both are handy and adept with their hands; each has a well-equipped woodworking shop in his basement. During adolescence, Carl rebuilt his Triumph GT6 auto, motor and all; Mark built large, radio-controlled airplanes. As their father, I would like to claim that the apple does not fall far from the tree. Alas, my sons inherited these "hands-on" genes from the distaff side of the family, for I quake at the prospect of changing a light bulb.

Both daughters also have professional careers. Alissa is a financial consultant, Mayela, a social worker. While both are athletic, Alissa is petite and almost dainty. She shocked her parents when we heard her blood-curdling cries as she fiercely contested her opponent in her karate class at Union College. We looked at each other in surprise wondering whether she was, indeed, our daughter. It came as less of a surprise to watch Mayela compete in a triathalon where she swam, biked and ran, outshining some of the older male competitors.

As with our sons, differences and similarities could be observed between our two daughters. When they were young, we videotaped their reactions to rock and roll music. Alissa moved gracefully, projecting an air of decorum by making small, controlled gestures with legs and arms. Mayela, upon hearing the heavy beat of the music, went wild with abandonment, undulating her body to the point of making us wonder if we had sired a future go-go dancer. At a college parents' weekend, Mayela and I danced together and handily won the lindy hop contest.

When we played rock and roll music, our two sons also reacted differently. Carl looked and acted cool; he moved to the beat like a young Michael Jackson. Mark's response was startling to behold; he threw himself in the air, landed on his back and spun around on the floor like a top. His response seemed to anticipate a rage that took hold some years later, break dancing.

Wintertime, there were numerous activities to be enjoyed near our home. One day, we took our two boys, who were preschoolers, to a skating pond. Huddled together in our VW to keep warm, Angela and I watched our sons perform on their first pairs of ice skates. Unsteady at first, they took running starts, reeled, spun in the air like Snoopy doing a dance, and ended up sprawled every which way on the ice. Rebounding quickly from their face-up or face-down positions, they were back on their feet for a repeat performance. Each time they wiped out, they laughed with glee. Watching them through the car window, we convulsed with laughter. Our only regret was not having taken along our movie camera.

The next time we returned to the pond, we were prepared and photographed their ice skating antics. Even though only a second try, they had already become more skilled and didn't fall as frequently or dramatically. But that didn't stop them from clowning around and wrestling with each other on the ice. Watching that video is like seeing Charlie Chaplin's silent film, *The Skating Rink.*

Summertime, we traveled to the Adirondacks to go mountain climbing. My brother-in-law was our skilled guide. But the one who took the lead, going up and down the mountains like a goat, was Carl. Five years old, he was indefatigable. On one climb, when I was at the point of collapse, Carl decided he needed a rest. As I thanked the mountain gods for this reprieve, I painfully lowered myself to the ground anticipating a long siesta. This was not to be. No sooner had I settled into a comfortable position than Carl was on his feet ready to go again. I resolved, then and there, to cut back on his trail-mix rations.

A child's job is to play. What our children enjoyed playing most was "Monster." In this game, sometimes two, other times three of them not yet in the first grade, scurried to find hiding places. With some audible sniffing of the air and groaning (the way the giant sounded when he was looking for Jack before he escaped down the beanstalk), I, the monster, called out that I was looking for children to take back to my lair. When I discovered an arm protruding from under the bed, or a leg sticking out of the clothes hamper, I captured and carried one or more of the squiggling bodies back to the bedroom where I entangled my victims in my arms and legs.

I then pretended to sleep and began to snore, all the while feeling legs and arms making slight movements to get free without disturbing the monster's sleep. Slowly, I lessened my hold until one body after another broke free and went squealing out of the room to find another hiding place. They never tired of this game and I wonder who had more fun, the monster or the hideaways.

All four children vividly remember a winter game in Central Park in Schenectady. In a small arena where they hold summer concerts, a space that is abandoned in winter, I invented this game—if you can call it a game. With snow piled up on all sides of the arena, I drove our VW around and around the open area as if I were operating a miniature army tank. Our two boys, stationed on the snow banks, lobbed snow balls at the car as I spun around and around the snowy surface to avoid their missiles. Occasionally, a snow ball would come through the open window, which brought gales of laughter from my daughters seated in the "toaster" of the car. I had my own store of ammunition next to the driver's seat and flung snowballs back, but with little accuracy.

In retrospect, this idea of children's play was insane but our kids loved it and I felt confident in controlling the spin of the car by keeping to the center of the arena. I am not surprised, however, that this activity does not appear in any parents' manual as suggested winter recreation for children.

Angela recalls an episode involving both boys, who were in elementary school at the time. This is an episode that has the eerie overtones of a tale from the pen of Edgar Allen Poe. One day, while helping Mark with his homework, Angela noticed that Carl was sitting at the bottom of the stairs looking downcast. She asked him several times if there was something wrong, but he gave no response. After repeated attempts to get him to answer, she put her arms around him and coaxed him into telling her what was the matter.

In a voice filled with sadness, Carl told his mother that while she was spending so much time with Mark, she was devoting little time to him, even though he was doing all his homework and getting good grades. Angela sought to reassure him and explained that Mark needed extra help. To reinforce this point, she said to Carl, "Suppose you were the father of two kids and one kid had only one leg. Wouldn't you give that kid extra help?" Angela embraced Carl once again and from his expression, she knew that he understood.

Some thirty years later, Carl telephoned that his wife, Jeanine, had given birth to their second son. In the midst of describing the details of the childbirth, Carl mentioned that Nicolai had been born with only one leg. According to Angela's memory, Carl reminded her of the story she had told him when he was a young boy. He reassured her that he would do as she had done, give his son all the extra help he needed. Not that Nicolai is pampered. Hopping around on his one leg, or using crutches when he is not wearing a prosthesis, at five years old, Nicolai is a gymnast, fearless in wrestling with his father and older brother, and a whirlwind of motion on the soccer field.

When I was at work, Angela did not resort to the game of making Dad the bad guy by telling the children, "Wait until your father gets home!" She took direct disciplinary action when it was necessary. I remember with some regret coming home from work to routinely ask thirteen-year-old Mark if he had done his homework. This constant reminder undermined the efforts he made to keep up with his school work. Angela alerted me as to how I was making a bad situation worse. I should have had more faith in an offspring who later proved he could do what had to be done in all subsequent endeavors.

Our minister related the story of how, when he was still a youngster, he showed his father, a Jewish immigrant from Europe, the grade of 95 he had received on a test. His father's response was, "They don't give out 100s any more?" Hearing this story, I was amused but, also, regretful for not having been more thoughtful as a parent.

In the course of collecting material for this autobiography, I asked my children, now adults, what special memories they have of growing up. Alissa recalls the following event which left a strong imprint upon her memory and character:

"One of the best ways I was able to show my mother all of the things she had taught me was to arrange a forty-fifth surprise birthday party for her with the help of my father and a friend. Thirty people came. I cleaned the house, decorated it and prepared food for our guests. I made all of my mother's special dishes: roasted peppers, ceviche, chicken cacciatore, sauteed mushrooms, poppyseed cake and lemon cake. My mother was pretty proud of me. I was eleven years old."

Mayela's description of one Thanksgiving dinner brought back another sweet memory:

"*Throughout the day, family and relatives arrived bringing with them much warmth and love. By mid-afternoon all the preparations for the Thanksgiving dinner were complete. Twenty-one people sat down at two long tables joined by a single tablecloth. The plentiful variety of food was laid out on the elegantly arranged table. We filled our glasses for a toast.*

My brother spoke for us all in hoping that we would continue in good health and would be together again soon. The sight of the shimmering candles and the sound of voices exchanging toasts filled me with a sense of warmth.

The end of the meal, hours later, left everyone in good spirits. My aunt, who was born in Spain, asked us if our bellies were shiny, an expression she had once used as a little girl after realizing that she had eaten too much.

As we waited for my father to give a short concert on the classical guitar, I looked around the room and thought about how proud I was to be part of this family. I knew we were not perfect and that all of us had our faults, but there were more things I liked than disliked about being 'Calabrese.'

The concert ended and we all danced. My parents did the lindy hop, a popular dance from the Big Band Era, and the rest of the family danced to disco music. Later, we lit a fire in the fireplace, roasted chestnuts and sat around talking in small groups. Perhaps it was the result of this being my last year to live at home before going to college, or perhaps, it was the happy combination of family, food and fun; but, whatever it was, it made this Thanksgiving Day one I will forever remember."

While our children were still in their teens, an elderly guest at a cocktail party proudly announced that he had four grandchildren. I quipped, "We don't have any grandchildren, but we do have four great children!" Now that our children are grown and have children of their own, I see no reason to change my appraisal. All four children are a source of much pride to their father who needs to bite his tongue when the conversation turns to how the younger generation has gone to the dogs.

Having written about our children, I must acknowledge that at the core of my life is my wife, Angela. What puzzles me is that authors dedicate their works to their wives and, yet, write so sparingly about them. I will speak at some length about my wife and trust the reader will forgive my indulgence.

In my marriage, I have to keep reminding myself of the words of Marcel Proust who wrote: "The real voyage of discovery consists not in seeking new landscapes but in having new eyes." How to continue to have new eyes in my marriage? How to see my wife not only in the world of worries and bills, fears and pain, but also, in her sacred aspects, from the point of view of eternity, to see her as a goddess, a madonna?

Angela's name is suitably chosen, for she has more than a little in common with angels honored in Christian mythology. Within the world of myth, I could compare her to the Virgin Mary, revered and exalted above all other women in Catholicism. However, the richness and complexity of her personality is better mirrored in the poetic, animated images of Greek mythology than in any book of psychology or theology with which I am familiar.

Like Hera, the beautiful queen of the goddesses, Angela values, first and foremost, the marriage bond and family life. She is a warm and caring person who can intuit when to help and when not to. Unlike Hera, she is level-headed and adaptive and rarely goes off in a rage. Of course, I have not philandered like Zeus, not merely out of conscience but for fear of her wrath.

Like Aphrodite, Angela prizes beauty in all its forms. As an alchemical goddess, she attempts, and sometimes succeeds, in transforming baser metals (my character and personality) into gold or, at least fools' gold. Following my lead, she has become extrovertive and enjoys the company of others. Without a doubt, she is a sensual woman who will break out in a belly dance at the slightest suggestion of my amorous intent. She eats with gusto and is not above using her fingers instead of a fork to make direct contact with food that cries to be picked up. She laughs readily at my wit which has inspired me to see the humor in life.

Like Athena, the goddess of wisdom and the arts, her ability to think well, to solve practical problems and strategize continues to amaze me. She is her father's daughter, and is always up to the task of solving mechanical problems in our home. Her prudence has brought me down to earth after my Icarus flights in the sky. Self-assertive when she needs to be, her warrior power is in the interest of peace.

Like Hestia, the oldest and most sacred of the twelve great Olympians, the goddess of the hearth fire who presides over domestic life, Angela cooks nutritious meals which keep me healthy, as well as all of my favorite Italian dishes which keep me happy. In addition, and without fanfare, she tends the altar fires by making a temple of our home. Intuitive, not given to solitude, she embodies spirit as well as soul.

Like Demeter, earth goddess par excellence, Angela personifies the Great Mother archetype. Her children and grandchildren are a primary focus in her life. Her Persephone is not one but two daughters whom she is ready to help at a moment's notice. It is easy for me to become dependent upon her, for she is willing to help and give generously of her time and energy.

Angela remembers going through a "blue period" after the birth of our first child; she became nervous and concerned about whether she would be a good mother. With the birth of our second child, that worry had vanished. I have never known another woman who filled the role of mother with as much heart and soul.

While we reacted to our children based on their individual needs, when it it came to discipline, we attempted to use a code that treated them similarly. During those years when sibling rivalry reached a peak, our sons would tease each other and play rough to the point of hurting one another. Angela acted as referee for their bouts but, one day, having reached the limits of her patience, she let them continue fighting without intervening and then announced that it was her turn.

For the first and last time, she gave both boys a strapping after which all three had a good cry. That night when they were sleeping, she could hear their sighs and it broke her heart. She felt sorry for being so harsh with them and having lost control of her temper. However badly she felt, her intervention was effective; that was the last time they teased or provoked each other. Today, as men, they are close friends.

Like Artemis, the moon goddess, Angela has been fertile in giving birth and direction to our children and in healing sickness in whatever form it befalls any member of our family, near or far. For twenty years, she cared for her mother at our home until her mother died, and also helped her mother's brother in his remaining years. She sets her own goals and usually reaches them. Not a proclaimed feminist, she forms friendships with women, is independent, and knows what she wants and how to get it.

Like Persephone, she dances on light feet so that flowers bloom everywhere, indoors and out. Always receptive to new ideas and skills, she appreciates a fertile imagination in whatever form it takes.

Angela drinks herbal tea out of a mug which reads: "FIRST GOD CRE-ATED MAN - THEN HE HAD A BETTER IDEA." No doubt, whoever created Angela came up with an original idea. The Creator fashioned a Renaissance woman: sculptor, painter of Chinese scrolls, creator of a Japanese Garden, ballroom dancer par excellence, tennis player, interior decorator, seamstress, barber, handy-woman, editor for this book, and a first-rate cook. Her art and life are one.

At my 70th birthday celebration, Mayela introduced a game called "Hammer and Spoon." Angela and I sat in two chairs, back to back; we each held a hammer in one hand and a spoon in the other. So positioned, we were barraged by a series of questions: "Who is the neatest?", "Who is the better driver?", "Who is the better dancer?", "Who is the most intelligent?", "Who is the better lover?", "Who makes the decisions in the family?", etc. In response to each question, we each raised either the hammer or the spoon—the hammer signified me, the spoon, Angela.

I raised my hammer as the neatest, the better driver and lover and lit-tle else. Our dual response to each question brought boisterous laughter and comments. What amazed both participants and spectators alike was the universal agreement in our responses. After four decades of marriage, it seems that, as husband and wife, we had come to recognize each other's virtues and limitations.

When family and friends were encouraged to each ask a question of his or her own, one asked, "Who is the luckiest in the marriage?" Instantly and simultaneously, I raised my hammer and Angela raised her spoon.

Now that our children are grown and have their own families, I have gained a new identity—"Granddad," alias "Poppie," alias "Pop Pop." With this new status, I have had an an opportunity to broaden and deepen my learning in ways I had not anticipated. I have relearned old games and invented new ones, for example, the Monster game with a wrinkle. I tell the hideaways that they can control the monster by holding any object in their hands and that by thrusting it at the monster's face, they can stop him dead in his tracks. I find that our grandchildren take great delight in seeing the monster contort his features and cringe as they hold up their magic object; they parade before him with impunity. They can control the monster until he breaks the spell and goes chasing after them.

Playing Monster is one game in which I can claim superiority over their grandmother. When she tried being the monster, she was informed by one grandson, "No, it's not the same...boring!" It gives me a sense of pride to know that I make a better monster than Nana.

On one recent trip to visit our offspring, I was greeted by my four-year-old grandson, Kyle, who eagerly took me by the hand and said that we had to go mosquito hunting. Not feeling particularly spry after four hours of driving, hunting mosquitoes was not a challenge uppermost in my mind. But I went along anyway on the afternoon mosquito patrol that my grandson had planned.

Acting as guide, Kyle led me warily toward the canopy of trees and ominous-looking bushes behind the house. It was a sunny afternoon and before we climbed into the backyard treehouse, I fashioned a five-foot bow and several arrows out of the surrounding bushes—effective weapons should we encounter any blood-sucking hordes that had the temerity to cross our path. With an assortment of sticks and branches, we began to set ingenious traps to capture our prey. I lost all sense of time and it was only when I saw my spouse heading in our direction that I looked at my watch. Two hours had lapsed.

Angela called me aside and handed me a book on the stars and constellations, substantial fare for man and boy to sink their teeth into. Somewhat reluctant to break the enchantment of our mosquito hunt, but feeling a tinge guilty that I might be neglecting the proper education of our grandson, after his grandmother left on her well-intentioned visit, I proceeded to give our preschooler a lesson in astronomy.

I called up to Kyle in the tree house and asked if he knew about the Big Dipper. Responding in an off-handed way, his voice betraying a small measure of irritation, he patiently proceeded to reel off, as far as I know, every extant fact known about the Big Dipper. Recovering from my amazement at his erudition, I tried, once again, to continue our astronomy lesson.

I called up to the tree house and asked him about the Little Dipper. Not only was I barraged with facts about the Little Dipper, but was informed about how other stars constellated into the figure of a giant bear. Big Dipper or Little Dipper, my grandson knew more about astronomy than I had ever known. Feeling somewhat sobered by what I had experienced, I asked myself, "How did I pass myself off as a college professor all these years?" Was I, in fact, an impostor? Dismissing this train of thought, I closed the book and decided to get back to serious business: PLAY. Granddad and grandson went back to mapping out new strategies to catch any mosquitoes foolhardy enough to come within a five-mile range.

With the afternoon waning, we walked back to the house and I suddenly realized how youthful and energized I felt. On the way up the path, Kyle looked up at me and said, "I love you, Granddad!"

CHAPTER ELEVEN

▼

TEACHING AND COMING
ALIVE IN THE CLASSROOM

*Is that what they call a vocation, what you do with joy as if you had
fire in your heart, the devil in your body?*

Josephine Baker

It is truly mysterious how some people at an early age seem to know
what they want to be when they grow up, their vocation. In my early
teens, after spending Saturday afternoons at the movies, I alternated
between wanting to be a cowboy, a detective and a musketeer. The
thought that I would someday be a teacher never entered my mind.

But there were signs in my youth of having a calling. In the fourth grade, I was chosen to be the art teacher's helper; as an adolescent, I organized a weight-lifting club. When my cousins visited, I would leave my room briefly to greet them, then return to my studies. Returning from school, each day, I completed my homework before going out to play.

Throughout my life, I have loved reading, whether it be novels and essays, or books on philosophy and psychology. I could brag and say that I am proud of my extensive library were it not for the fact that, unhappily, I have not read all of the books in it. Not only have I not succeeded in ridding myself of books I will probably never read, but I keep buying more books. You might as well know I am an addict as far as books are concerned.

When I look back at my childhood, though, it does seem unlikely that I would end up a teacher. I was slow to speak and when I did, I developed a lisp. There were no books in our home. I never thought of myself as bright, nor did I think my family regarded me as having any special talent. I knew myself to be a late developer; it seemed I always had to work hard to do well. But compensating for these limitations was a trait I did have—perseverance. In elementary school, on every report card I received an "A" for effort.

My formal career as a teacher began when I received a one-year appointment at the State Teachers College at Albany (later to become the State University of New York at Albany). During that first trial by fire, I remember teaching graduate and undergraduate courses by the book. My insecurity forbade me from doing otherwise.

My next teaching appointment was at Russell Sage, a small liberal arts college for women in Troy, New York. While I kept initially to the traditional format of lecture and discussion, classroom demonstrations and showing films, I soon began to loosen up. After several years of teaching, the following description appeared in the *Russell Sage College Year Book:*

"The enthusiasm and obvious zest for living which characterizes Dr. Calabria are felt from the first moment's acquaintance with him. He instills in even the most apathetic student a sense of search and discovery through his dynamic classroom discussions. A dedicated man, a man who gives his all to whatever he does, Dr. Calabria is a distinctive asset to the College. He finds joy in successful teaching and strives toward attaining ever higher goals for his students and for himself. He is never unwilling to allow a class discussion to stray onto an interesting tangent and seeks to give each student opportunity for expression through individual conferences. The presence of this energetic mustachioed gentleman brings a refreshing awareness and vigor to the faculty."

I was shocked when I was passed over for promotion to Associate Professor while a more recent member of the department received this appointment. I confronted the president, who responded bluntly and to the point. If I did not like being at the college, I should look elsewhere. From the outset, I felt ill-at-ease with the authoritarian stance of the college administration.

Given this ultimatum, I was severely distressed. I was forty years old, with a family of three children and another on the way. A new teaching position would not be easy to locate, not with my meager track record in publications. The thought of uprooting my family filled me with much anxiety. I decided to swallow my pride and stay on. What made my stay bearable was the congeniality of colleagues and the responsive student body.

But my psyche would not let me forget what I regarded as unfair treatment. My unconscious reflected my unsettled state of mind through a number of dreams that bordered on nightmares. Two dreams are classic examples of Freudian wish-fulfillment. Unlike the outcome in the following dreams, in real life, I was not the victor but the vanquished.

David and Goliath

I am throwing stones at a giant, who hurtles large boulders back which I have to dodge. One of the stones I hurl catches the monster in the pit of the stomach and bowls him back and causes him to retreat to a cave.

Usurper to the Throne

The setting is a mythical kingdom where a dictator has kept the people under his rule. His subjects have made several attempts to overcome his domination but are unsuccessful. The rightful prince to the throne is pursued by several henchmen who try to kill him. In trying to defend the prince, I am wounded, but keep hammering at the head of one henchman, and my blows finally bring him down.

During my stay at Russell Sage, I made a number of friends, two of whom are forever memorable. One such colleague, Bob Browne, in the sociology department, impressed me with his passion for ideas and the masterful way he drew upon concepts from the social sciences and humanities. He became my intellectual mentor. Dissatisfied with the college administration, he left after a brief stay.

Although Bob's appointment was in the sociology department, his scholarly passions were in the fields of philosophy and religion. He wrote a master's thesis on Zen Buddhism. Were I to identify him with one of the ancient Greek gods, it would be with Apollo, the god of light and rational order, the god of enlightenment. Bob broadened and deepened my perspective on both religion and psychology by introducing me to the ideas of theologians Martin Buber and Paul Tillich, and to psychologists Carl Jung and Erich Fromm. On summer weekends, we would sit on a park bench overlooking Lake George in upstate New

York and trade our understanding of these fertile minds. While the setting was tranquil, our discussions were animated.

Even after Bob moved to a college in the mid-west, we kept in close touch. We met periodically, talked over the phone occasionally, and exchanged letters frequently. Bob continued to reply using pencil and yellow-lined paper while I made use of my typewriter. Had a quill and parchment been readily available, I am certain Bob would have preferred this mode of transcription.

After he retired from teaching, Bob contented himself with writing an occasional paper, not for the purpose of publication, but to answer a request from a local organization interested in the world of ideas. One morning, not long after his seventieth birthday, Bob quietly passed away. I am sure that, as I write, he is engaging some philosopher or saint in spirited dialogue in the great beyond.

Alex Rymanowski, a student in one of my classes in the Continuing Education Program, approached me at the end of one semester and asked if I would be interested in listening to a jazz group playing at a local club. From that time and for the next twenty years, we maintained the closest of friendships. In fact, Alex was my best friend.

A Polish-American, Alex felt a kinship with Dionysus and his companion Eros. At ease with people, Alex savored the world through his senses and relied on his intuition as much as reason in making decisions. During the work week, he functioned as a manager in a company which manufactured 3M Tape. On weekends, Alex played the saxophone and clarinet and sang in a polka band he and his brother had started.

We both shared a passion for music, food and wine. I invited Alex to my home and everyone in the family fell in love with him. A visit from Alex became an event in our household, a time for celebration. One day, my four-year-old daughter Alissa answered the door when he rang the bell. Towering above her, Alex bent down and asked, "Can your father come out and play?"

Playtime at our home took on many forms. One day, our two young daughters mischievously performed a striptease for Alex's benefit. Another time, Mayela, our brashest offspring and a clone of the great dancer Isadora Duncan, draped herself over his lap in a seductive pose. Alex picked her up and handed her to me commenting, "I can't handle her!"

On Saturday afternoons, Alex acted as our family guide, leading us across a shallow part of the Mohawk River to reach a bunch of rocks nestled in the flowing river. In this primitive setting near where he lived, we frolicked to our hearts' content. Standing upright on one of these rocks, Alex reminded me of an Indian brave, one from the tribe of the Mohawk Indians who once inhabited this region. As he smoked his big cigar, drank red wine, feasted on Italian bread, sausages, mozzarella and black olives, he replied to my questions about the region's history with a solitary, "Ugh!"

Like Pablo, in Herman Hesse's novel *Steppenwolf*, who plays the saxophone and acts as a guide to the professor, Alex was my mentor. In the framework of Jungian psychology, Alex represented my shadow, my dark side, a side which we must all recognize and honor at our peril. I introduced him to the writings of existentialists like Kafka, Camus, Sartre and deBeauvoir. In turn, he shared his enthusiasm for American expatriate Henry Miller and the poet Dylan Thomas. Raised in a small town with immigrant Polish parents, Alex worked his way up the social ladder. He became the first one in his family to graduate from college. When I met him, he had begun courting the mayor's daughter and ran for town alderman, losing the election by a few votes.

One day, Alex went to his office at 3M with a collage he had made with the company's product. He hung his artwork on the wall behind his desk. His attempt at innovation did not sit well with his superiors. Tension between Alex and management escalated, making work almost unbearable for Alex. He finally left his job and went off to France for a vacation. When he returned, although jobless, he was exuberant and filled with a sense of life.

When his savings were gone, Alex went seeking work but became dissatisfied with every position he found. He began to see himself as the existential man he had read about, alienated from himself and the world. I saw the changes he was going through and felt helpless to reverse his downward cycle as he fluctuated between euphoria and depression.

Just before reaching his fiftieth birthday, Alex suffered a fatal heart attack. The night before this tragedy, he played the saxophone and clarinet with great intensity at the Polish Community Center. It was as though like his favorite poet, Dylan Thomas, he "raged against the night." His wife, whom he had married in his forties, asked me to be a pallbearer. The weight of the casket cut into my shoulders and I felt as if I were Christ bearing the cross. The night before the burial, the funeral parlor was jammed with family and friends. Alex never realized how much he was loved.

I did not see the end coming, though I might have had some intimation from two events before his heart attack. A month before he died, Alex entrusted to me two loose-leaf binders which he said he wanted me to have. They were a collection of observations he had made over the years. Initially, I put them aside as I prepared for end-term examinations.

The second event happened one week before he died. After an evening meal at our home, as he left me at the curb before driving away in his VW bug, he embraced me and told me how much our relationship meant to him. Even as I think back to that meeting—his final goodbye—there is a catch in my throat and my eyes begin to tear.

As a tribute to our friendship, I would like to share some trenchant observations he recorded in one of these notebooks, called *Punches and Jabs (Round One)*. He signed his work *Alex Pepper*, and wrote in the preface, "This book was actually written by a 'ghost writer'—the ghost within me that refuses to be put down." And his final wry admonition: "THIS IS A BOOK FOR MATURE AUDIENCES. NON-PARENTAL DISCRETION IS ADVISED."

From two-hundred pages with some six entries on each page, here are a dozen of his observations:

"What a terrible year 1977 was! We lost three legends—Groucho Marx, Zero Mostel and Charlie Chaplin. Is GOD planning some GRAND PLAY?"

"Plumbers are the real cause of Pornography. So help me.They freely and legitimately use terms like brass cocks; love joy couplings; female sweat adapters; extra heavy black nipples; and deep throat clamps."

"'Bleak' is really a funny word. Think about it. 'Bleak.'"

"Me afraid of death? Nah. Not much. Christ, I still have to deal with that sense of finality I experience when mailing a letter. Know what I mean? Like KLUNK. It's gone—never see it again."

"That, my fellow philosophers, is part of a true Existential feeling. Just play it by ear. Hell! There are better erogenous zones than that!"

"Warning: The Surgeon General Has Determined That Smoking Is Dangerous To Your Health. So is Life."

"That statue of Atlas holding up the World without a jock frightens me."

"Bashful. Doc. Sleepy. Grumpy. Dopey. Sneezy. Happy. Seven great little guys who made the best of their situation and never underwent analysis."

"The thing I like so much about kites, aside from flying them, is that they make you look up."

"Strange, but I have yet to see a portrait of Christ smiling. Have you? If so, please mail it to me."

"I am the only one who has discovered the unique element to all mankind. Quite a statement, hey? Well, the element is the common sneeze, AH-CHOO! Why? Because if you think about it, have you ever heard anyone sneeze CHOO-AH?"

"What a beautiful day! Remind me to put God back on my birthday list."

I left Russell Sage College after a seven-year stay. It seemed pure serendipity how, just prior to my confrontation with the president, a student in one of my evening division classes suggested I invite to my class Prof. Clare Graves from the psychology department at nearby Union College. I shared an interest with Prof. Graves in the works of psychologist Abraham Maslow. It was, no doubt, through Graves' recommendation that I received an appointment to Union College, where I remained for twenty-three years before retiring. At Union College, I came into my own as a teacher. On the Union campus during the tumultuous years of the sixties and seventies, I was known, unofficially, as "Crazy Frank," for reasons to be revealed ahead.

Feeling a sense of freedom in my new surroundings, I trusted my intuition as to what felt right in teaching my courses. Following this inner voice, I was not always consciously aware of what I was doing, nor of the consequences that might follow. Within my first month of classes, on a beautiful autumn day, I perched myself in front of my students on the wide branch of the male ginkgo tree in Jackson's Garden located on the campus. It seemed a good vantage point from which to discuss the concept of power and authority, basic themes in my course in Social Psychology. Didn't Mussolini and Hitler position themselves on balconies above the crowds to make their demagogic speeches?

In the midst of my lecturing, waving my arms for effect as did these dictators, I was aghast to see Professor Huntley, Chairman of the Psychology Department, peering at me through the garden railing. Though the branch of the ginkgo tree was stout, when I saw his look of amazement, I felt as shaky as a fiddler on the roof. That evening, when I returned home, my instruction to my wife was brief: "Pack!" Fortunately, Prof. Huntley must have regarded my style of teaching as quirky, but not totally unprofessional, for there were no negative repercussions.

I found the students at Union industrious, capable and a delight to teach. The solid reputation that Union College has always enjoyed is due, in large measure, to the students it attracts, as well as to its praiseworthy faculty. I felt privileged to be a member of this venerable institution of learning which recently celebrated its two-hundredth anniversary.

When I first joined the Union College faculty in 1966, a spirit of change was in the air. In 1966, the Vietnam War had escalated and the monthly draft calls shot up almost tenfold over 1965's figures of 5,000 per month. Campuses erupted in protest when the Johnson administration, in order to fill quotas, abolished blanket student deferments; many college students were then reclassified.

In an article titled "The College Scene: What's Happening?" written for *Symposium, the Union College Quarterly*, I described what I perceived to be the tenor of the times as reflected on college campuses in America. Here are two excerpts from that article:

"In a decade of happenings, the 'Love Children,' America's home-grown 'hippies,' expressed their views on all kinds of volatile issues through the simple, direct medium of lapel buttons which read: 'Turn On, Tune In, Drop Out,' 'Jesus was a dropout,' 'Draft beer, not students,' 'Burn pot, not people,' 'Flower power,' 'The Great Society: Bombs...Bullets...Bull,' 'Ban the Bra,' 'Don't Trust Anyone Over Thirty,' 'We Shall Overcome,' 'God is on a Trip,' 'Make Love Not War,' 'Keep The Faith Baby,' 'Warning: Your Local Police are Armed and Dangerous,' 'Suppose They Gave A War And Nobody Showed Up?;'I am a Human Being: Do Not Fold, Spindle or Mutilate!'

In their quest for depth the young college generation, more fully aware than ever of the omnipresence of death through wars, violence, and destruction, are attempting to rediscover the sense of play, as Huizinga means it, so as to leave 'no unlived lines' in the human body. The new music and dances, the experimentation with drugs and sex—in short, the attraction to the moving, the pulsating, often exaggerated sounds of the times, in preference to listening to a tired drummer sounding measured beats to a joyless existence—is perhaps what is happening."

One example of how the turmoil of the sixties surfaced at Union College took place during a graduation ceremony. The commencement speaker began his address to the class when, off to the side of the dais, a dissident group of men from off campus began to shout. One member of the group waved a Viet Cong flag. For a moment, there was confusion. But one professor was not confused. With a few leaps, he steeple-chased over several bushes and, with his academic regalia flying behind him like Superman's cape, pulled the flag from the student's hands and ran off with it.

I cheered, along with other members of the faculty, at the action taken by Professor Bick, a math professor also known for his marathon running. I had strong reservations, as did many college students, about our bankrupt policy in Viet Nam. When I thought about this episode later, it brought back a boyhood memory of playing "King of the Hill." Only that day on campus, a children's game had turned into a serious adult confrontation.

Rapid social change such as America was experiencing during the sixties called for change in the classroom to reach students who were both anxious and rebellious. The time was ripe for experimentation. I introduced a teaching approach I called "Theater of the Mind," which gave students an opportunity, through experiential learning, to participate directly in the learning process. Students, working in small groups, became the teachers. I was amazed to witness how seriously they took this role and how success-fully they engaged the other members of the class.

The idea for Theater of the Mind came from reading Hesse's novel, *Steppenwolf.* The main character is a professor whose education has been lopsided; he is a man who lives in his head (my own affliction). In the course of the novel, he meets a number of guides, both female and male, who teach him to cultivate his senses as he has cultivated his mind. One guide, Pablo, a jazz musician, introduces him to the Magic Theater. Over the door to the theater is a large sign: "FOR MADMEN ONLY—THE PRICE OF ADMISSION YOUR MIND—NOT FOR EVERYBODY."

Anticipating resistance from some students to this method of teaching psychology, and anticipating questions my colleagues might raise about this classroom procedure, I sought to lessen everyone's anxiety, including my own, by assigning readings from a standard text and testing the class on standard examinations. Once the subject matter of the text had been covered in the first half of the semester using a traditional format, I introduced Theater of the Mind.

I first used the format of Theater of the Mind in my class in History and Systems of Psychology. The subject matter called for tracing how psychology evolved, from its early connections to philosophy to a modern-day science. I found much of the material dry and hard to digest. I needed to come up with a way to present the material that would hold the students' interest.

The class was divided into groups of threes. Each group had to present a class in which they dramatized how the concept of the unconscious appeared in the history of psychology in whatever guise. They were to choose one of the following cultures in their research: Primitive, Egyptian, Judaic-Christian, Greek, African, Oriental, European or Indian (both Asian and North American). I directed their attention to a gold mine of information: myths, rituals, symbols, legends, fairy tales and shamanistic practices. At the end of each group's presentation, those who "taught" the class had to engage their classmates in discussion.

Here is what happened in one class presentation. The group chose to do research on the American Indian. They used the resources of the Union College and Schenectady libraries to obtain both audio and written material. The program began with an introduction to the legends and myths of the Iroquois, folk tales having to do with how the world came about, and the relationship between man and nature. Then the trio sprang into action. One student, in loin cloth, his body painted, danced to a recording coming from two large speakers turned up to full volume. He circled around and around a pan of lighted kerosene placed on the floor. Not a skilled dancer, at one point he accidentally tipped over the pan and singed the carpet in the classroom.

Between the volume of sound and the momentary sight of fire, I felt unnerved and for good reason. The dean's office was right outside the door of the classroom. Though I had tenure, I feared for my advancement in the college. The gods to which the students chanted may have heard my prayer and called the dean elsewhere while this class was going on.

Theater of the Mind reversed my position in the classroom. I became the pupil; the students became the teachers. For example, I learned from the presentation on the American Indian that the Iroquois had developed a sophisticated understanding of dreams that predated Freud's discoveries by centuries.

I was both amazed and pleased with the scholarship and inventiveness of the students who presented this program. Other class presentations matched this level of scholarship and dramatic skill. Despite the time the class met, 8:30 in the morning, few students came late and fewer still missed a class. I gave one grade to all members of the group so as to discourage any laggards. It seemed that getting a high grade on these assignments was not of uppermost concern. It was as if the students' direct involvement in the learning experience was its own reward.

On the last day of classes, I had the students fill out an unsigned questionnaire to record their responses and suggestions for improving this teaching approach.

All the students reported that these programs took a good deal of time and energy to prepare. Here was one typical response: "I felt that we, as a group (as well as myself, as an individual) had created something worthwhile...because our minds had united in the task at hand, there were three times as many ideas with which to work."

When I had the opportunity to submit suggestions for new course offerings, my wish list read: Humanistic Psychology, The Psychology of Creativity, and Psychology Through Literature. What joy it was the following year when I was given permission to teach all three courses!

Preparing for these courses, I felt like a young boy in Macy's Toy Department during the Christmas season. By attending conferences on humanistic psychology and sensitivity and encounter group workshops at growth centers, I had a wealth of material to draw upon for the classroom.

From a toolbox of "psycho technologies," I selected a number of experiential exercises designed to increase personal and interpersonal awareness. These exercises included both traditional and non-traditional approaches to learning: journal-keeping, recording one's dreams, creative problem solving, guided imagery, body relaxation, value clarification, sensory awareness and a variety of ways to deepen interpersonal relationships.

I could hardly contain my excitement on the first class meeting of Humanistic Psychology. I distributed a detailed course outline which included a challenging reading list. Housekeeping details out of the way, we went to the Arts building next door.

With their books put aside, I instructed students to lie on the dance floor where I put them into a state of deep relaxation. Through guided imagery, we traveled to Greece where we met our guide, Zorba. I read a passage from Kazenzakis' novel, *Zorba The Greek*, in which Zorba tells his pupil how much dancing means to him—Zorba dances when he feels great joy and great sorrow. The soundtrack from the movie heightened the effect of the dialogue between the young man and his mentor. The novel reaches a climax when the pupil asks his teacher, "Zorba, teach me to dance!"

We returned via the imagination to Union, there to the crucial part of the class lesson. The class formed a circle. I taught the class Zorba's dance. The students threw themselves into movement and the noise level rose in proportion. There was much merriment and excitement as the students discovered they were no longer strangers to one another.

The class format in Humanistic Psychology, as was true of my course in The Psychology of Creativity, was meant to balance mind and body and to stir the imagination. I didn't know it at the time, but I was in tune with the cutting edge of "New Age" psychology.

Psychology of Creativity was a follow-up course to Humanistic Psychology. The focus in this course was two-fold: to uncover how we block ourselves from being creative, and to understand the central role of the imagination in the creative process. A basic premise of the course is that everyone is creative in some way and to some degree. We know this to be true from watching children play. It came as a surprise when I read several authoritative sources claim that, on average, we use as little as ten percent, and rarely more than 25 percent, of our creative potential.

I had a field day in assembling readings for my course in Psychology Through Literature. It was Freud who acknowledged that it was the writers, the novelists and poets, who had "discovered" the unconscious long before he began formulating his theories. Using three of the six standard approaches to literary criticism, Freudian, Jungian, and Existentialism, I chose selections for this course which included both ancient and modern readings. Sophocles and Eugene O'Neil both wrote great dramas about the Oedipus Complex.

I attempted to counter the image of "Crazy Frank" by dressing and acting conventionally outside the classroom. It is true that I let my hair grow a bit longer after arriving at Union, but it was far from shoulder length. Nor was my salt-and-pepper beard very different from those worn by other professors on the campus. Still, given my track record, had there been a contest for "Hippie Professor of the Month," I would have been in the running.

At my retirement party, members of my department treated me to a lunch and gave me a wooden plaque which, in part, read:

"In his 23 years at Union, Frank Calabria helped bring variety and excitement to the teaching of psychology. Frank encouraged his students to break out of old passive modes of thinking and to experiment with new directions."

When I turned fifty, I embarked on a second career as a psychotherapist. This decision was prompted by the realization that our children would soon be going to college and I needed to find a way to make this financially possible. I did not imagine that taking a massage workshop at a resort in the Catskill Mountains would launch me on this second career. The instructor was from the the Esalen Institute in Big Sur, California, the leading growth center in the United States. I had always wanted to learn massage and was elated that Big Sur had come to my doorstep.

On the Friday evening the program began, I was in for a surprise. I had imagined that the class might begin with learning how to give a class member a foot massage, and then work up to a back rub. That's not what happened. Seated comfortably in the large room of a cabin, along with fifteen other men and women, I sat expectantly waiting for the workshop to begin.

The instructor was a young, slim, attractive female, with short, blonde hair, who looked like the actress Helen Hunt. She gave us a brief orientation and then, unselfconsciously, proceeded to undress. Though I had been married seventeen years, the sight of an unfamiliar, attractive naked woman was something of a shock. If my attention may have momentarily wandered during her opening remarks, once she presented herself in this manner, I must acknowledge that she had my full attention.

With the workshop underway, we all followed the lead of our instructor and disrobed. The matter-of-fact way our teacher presented herself to the class made it seem right and natural to be naked before a group of strangers. Over the course of the weekend, we spent twenty-two hours learning a variety of strokes and how to apply them from head to toe. No one in the class stood out because of their fashionable attire for, at every meeting, we were buck naked.

When I arrived home, I opened the garage door and found a massage table Carl had made while I was away. Before I had left for the workshop, I had mentioned I would have to locate a table when I returned. The sight of the table triggered the memory of a Christmas when I was five. On that Christmas morning, my parents told me to go down to the basement for a surprise. There, in the middle of the room, was a shiny red wagon that Santa Claus had left.

The evening I returned from the workshop, I gave my wife a massage from head to toe for the better part of two hours. She was in bliss. For the next few months, I continued to give her the benefits of that weekend in the Catskills. I am ever-ready to respond to my wife's need for a back massage, since I lack the skills of a handyman.

On the same weekend as the massage workshop, and in the same location, a second workshop was in progress. Having some interest in Gestalt Therapy, I asked the instructor, my dinner companion, how I might train to become a Gestalt therapist. He recommended I enroll in the Los Angeles Gestalt Institute where his teacher, Dr. Resnik, was giving seminars. Within the year, I took two workshops with Dr. Resnik and other members of the Institute and received over a hundred hours of training.

My experiences at the Los Angeles Gestalt Institute convinced me that this approach to psychotherapy was cutting-edge. When I returned home, the means were at hand to continue my training—more synchronicity. For the first time, the Cleveland Gestalt Institute was beginning a two-year intensive training program for mental health professionals in the tri-cities area of Albany, Troy and Schenectady. I enrolled in this program, along with some two-dozen mental-health practitioners, psychiatrists, psychologists and social workers. Though older than everyone in class, I felt like the new kid on the block.

The Cleveland Gestalt Training Program met for twenty weekends each year, at various locations. There were five members on the faculty, all highly competent trainers—a psychiatrist, two psychologists and two social workers. The training program combined hands-on experience with the study of the principles of Gestalt Therapy. During each meeting, we had an opportunity to practice the role of both therapist and patient. As the patient, the problems we presented were real, sometimes urgent. As the therapist, we were critiqued by both the training staff and the members of our group. It was hard to fake or hide behind either role.

During one weekend meeting, we focused on "dream work." I volunteered to work on a dream that I had had in recent times, one that had me puzzled as to its meaning.

The Village Priest and the Cardinal

I am walking in a deserted section of town; there are long walls that stretch away to the right, as well as straight ahead. I look down these walls and also watch where I am stepping because there are ditches in the ground. At the end of a long stretch, I come upon a mob of people surging out of a building, which, later, I identify as a church.

I go into the building and find a large portrait on the wall and hear someone announce my family name, Calabria. I am surprised to learn that the distinguished-looking man in the painting has my name. His portrait is imposing, as though painted by Rembrandt or Velasquez. There is warmth in his smile, though his face has an expression of embarrassment in being the subject of a painting done in this grand style.

I go through a side door from the room where the painting hangs and find that there is a ceremony in process. It is a funeral mass. It seems that some old priest has died and I hear disparaging remarks about him because he tried to become a psychotherapist late in life, after he was fifty.

The funeral ceremony is ludicrous; a team of horses draws a carriage-hearse down the center isle of the church at high speed. The priests in attendance are dressed in bizarre costumes. I watch the drama with curiosity and amazement. I am aware that I am an onlooker, someone separate from what is happening. I have the sense that there is something phony about the whole setup.

Being lost, and aware of the ditches in my path, is an accurate description of how I felt when I began this intensive period of training in psychotherapy. Earlier in my life, I felt lost when I left the Catholic Church. My training supervisor pointed out that the old priest, who may represent my Italian heritage and Catholic upbringing during the early years, had taken me through my boyhood and adolescence, and had given me a foundation upon which to build. Yes, there were some absurdities connected with growing up Italian and Catholic, and there were scars. However, without the old priest there would be no man in the portrait. I was reminded that while the town people loved the old priest, they only admired and respected the Cardinal.

One of the trainers in the program, a female psychiatrist, suggested that perhaps one message in the dream was: "Be more emotional. Be more spontaneous. Be more into your body. BE MORE ITALIAN!"

In his hilarious book, *How To Survive an Italian Family*, Rick Detorie notes that Italian families teem with love, drama, aggravation, guilt and passion. To survive, he tells us, requires personal diligence, perseverance, a thick skin, unusual communication skills and a hearty appetite. In my case, what helped me survive was going into therapy.

When I first opened a private practice, I had few patients who were Italian-Americans. I was puzzled, since Schenectady has a large Italian population. I came to the conclusion that perhaps little had changed since I was a child. Then, if you had a personal problem, you were encouraged to talk with a relative, presumably someone wise, or see a priest. Neither being professionals, it was not likely that you obtained deep insight into your problem. I am happy to report that, with the changing times, Italian-Americans are more likely to seek help from a professional. Of course, a few of my relatives still agree with Woody Allen, who said, "I'm going to give my psychiatrist one more year, then I'm going to Lourdes."

CHAPTER TWELVE

▼

Aging, Character & New Explorations

Every time I think I am getting old, and gradually going to the grave, something else happens.

Lillian Carter

At the three-quarter-century mark, I am still not convinced that I *am old*, although I have a sneaking suspicion that I am *getting old*. That suspicion arises every time I go dancing and have to ice my back and knee when I return home. Still, I am grateful that I am still able to dance, so who's complaining?

When I retired, I did not connect this milestone with the idea that I was getting old. It was a balmy, autumn day as I was about to begin my thirtieth year of teaching. I remarked to my wife at breakfast, "How nice it would be to stay home and listen to music instead of meeting my classes!" From the day I began my career as a teacher, she had never heard me say such a thing. Without missing a beat, she replied, "Why don't you retire?"

The prospect of retirement made me aware of how fortunate I had been in choosing teaching as a life's work. Thomas Carlyle wrote, "Blessed is he who has found his work. Let him ask no other blessedness."

The thought of not having to structure my life around strict schedules was appealing. Sixty-four-years old, I could have continued teaching for at least a half-dozen more years. What ultimately lured me to an early retirement was the number of projects I was interested in exploring, and others that cried out for completion.

The prospect of visiting family and friends more often, and traveling to distant places I had never been, was another compelling reason for retiring. I would have more time to improve my dancing and play the guitar. There were books to be read and much music to be listened to. Besides, the house was paid for and the children were off and running. Angela and I could live comfortably on our savings and social security.

My fantasy of a retirement celebration was to have a large number of my students return from every state of the union to pay homage to me as they did in the movie classic, *Goodbye Mr. Chips*. Mr. Chips, modest soul that he was, was overwhelmed by this reception and ended up in tears.

Well, in my case, it didn't happen that way. In place of a farewell gathering of some 4,000 students I had taught, I did what old generals do, I silently faded away. When sanity and good reason replaced my run-away fantasies, I settled for the wish that should I meet a former student, he or she will not cross over to the other side of the street or pummel me on the sidewalk. Of course, I am gratified to hear from former students who tell me that I was one of their best professors.

While still a prisoner of my grandiose retirement fantasy, I imagined the courses I had introduced at Union would be part of the psychology curriculum for centuries to come. Alas, when I left, so did all the courses I had taught.

At first, I comforted myself with the rationalization that I was irreplaceable and, like some famous ballplayer whose number is retired after he leaves the game, there was little chance of finding a worthy successor. But the real reason for discontinuing my courses had more to do with the times and the changing interests of members of the psychology department.

A project of mine that cried for completion was a study of the dance marathon fad which had captured the fancy of large audiences during the manic 20s and the 30's Great Depression. I had begun my study of this phenomenon two decades earlier. One colleague remarked, "No one can accuse you of premature closure." Though I wanted to clobber him for that comment, I had to acknowledge that he was right. What kept me from completing this research was my attraction to each new approach which promised to be definitive. I was like a dog chasing his tail.

What triggered my interest in this subject was the film, *They Shoot Horses, Don't They?* After seeing the movie, I went directly to the Union College library to begin my research. Much of my information, however, came from spending countless hours at the dance library at the Lincoln Center for the Performing Arts in New York.

The notion that what one American can do, another can do longer, if not better, fueled this dance craze. The basement of American show business, this bastard form of entertainment, "A Poor Man's Nightclub," borrowed from vaudeville, burlesque, night club acts and sports. I documented the fact that, unlike most fads that had a longevity of six months, dance marathons lasted thirty years. Over these decades, some 20,000 contestants and show personnel participated - audiences consisted mainly of women.

With the help of several grants from Union College, I met with former contestants in tenement apartments in New Jersey, as well as in dark bars and well-lighted bungalows in the Hollywood, California area. Five years after beginning this project, I wrote an article on the history of dance marathons, which was published in the *Journal of Popular Culture*.

Three years after I left the classroom, I completed *Dance of the Sleepwalkers: The Dance Marathon Fad*, the first in-depth study of this craze. Bowling Green State University Popular Press published my book in 1993. Fully engaged in completing this project, the transition to retirement seemed painless, for I was doing what professors do on their sabbatical, researching and writing.

It seemed sheer masochism on my part to start another manuscript so soon after finishing the dance marathon project. Along with material on dance marathons, I had collected books and articles on dancing in its many forms written from different perspectives. My intention was to trace how social dancing through the ages revealed changes in the status and roles of men and women in society. I had barely completed a draft of the first chapter when I realized that I was writing more about my life than about social dancing. I followed my intuitive sense and switched my direction. However, had I known the challenging task ahead, I might never have begun what became a consuming passion, a labor of love. Unlike my previous literary experience, choosing to write an autobiography affected both my sleep and waking hours.

I have, over several decades, collected hundreds of my dreams. Freud found that our dreams express the irrational side of our personality; put directly, each night, we go quietly crazy. Jung noted that in our dreams, we are more rational than in our waking state; we can draw upon the collective unconscious, a repository of the wisdom of the ages.

Many of our dreams have scripts reminiscent of those found on afternoon soap-operas and evening sitcoms, as well as in myths and legends.

The name I have given to each of the following dreams is meant to identify a core theme: *An Archeological Dig, The Blind Boy,* and *The*

Reluctant Artist, my search for an identity; *The Vampire* and *Meeting The Godfather,* my meeting the dark, shadow-side of myself; *Guitar Unstrung, Broken Statue,* and *The Man in the Splint,* the challenges which come with aging.

When I began writing my autobiography, the content of a number of my dreams took on a different quality.

Celebration of Light

I am in a church where a festive ceremony is underway. I am awed by the rituals being enacted on the altar by men in white vestments. Alongside the altar, a troop of black dancers performs as though at a Mardi Gras festival.

I am amazed when a carnival of animals enters the church. The animals look over the railing at the people on the altar. The scene reminds me of Rousseau's painting, "Innocence."

The church is bathed in light. I say to myself, "This is what a ritual celebration should be like!"

After I awakened from this dream, I felt a sense of freedom, a sense of creation, the challenge to reinvent myself.

Light Bearers

I am in a dark place. I am able to keep a large circle of varicolored lights glowing like the red-hot embers of a fire. I enjoy keeping the lights on with such intensity, though I don't know how I am able to do this. I notice that, nearby, someone is doing what I am doing. At times, the glow from his light is radiant, and, at other times, the brilliance is dampened. There is a third person present. He is a teacher, a guru. He tells me that the spirit is like the light. Only when the spirit is pure can the intensity of the light suffuse us.

Reflecting on this dream with its extraordinarily vivid colors, I found the following words from the *Cabala,* an ancient mystical doctrine, instructive: "We receive the light and then we impart it, and thus, we repair the world."

Horizons

I am standing on a wooden platform on the porch of the house in which I grew up. I hold the hand of a small girl as she climbs up and down the stairs going from the platform to the sidewalk, a considerable feat for one so small. I walk her around the platform and feel a sense of pride.

The branches of a large magnolia tree which stands in front of the house have been trimmed, allowing me to have a clear view of the Narrows, the body of water which separates Brooklyn from Staten Island. Off to the left of the platform is a crow's next which affords me an even broader view of the horizon.

It feels great to be standing on the platform, looking out at the sea, and having the fresh breezes blow in my face.

With retirement, I had begun to widen my perspective, previously narrowed by focusing on job and family. This dream may be telling me that, in this stage of my life, I will have to regain the uncluttered vision of the child. Jung writes, "In every adult there lurks a child—an eternal child, something that is always becoming, is never completed and calls for unceasing care, attention and education. That is the part of the human personality which wants to develop and become whole."

Diamonds in the Sky

I am in a spacious place. The sky has a deep, blue color. Floating in the sky is a luminous box which keeps dissolving and reappearing. The box is like a many-sided diamond with convex and concave surfaces. As it tumbles in the sky, the box gives off flashes of light.

The holographic imagery of this dream was so powerful that I felt like Luke Skywalker in a *Star Wars* movie. Perhaps this dream was say-ing: *Trust the force; trust your intuition, your inner voice, your soul.* My reflections about the many-sided diamond included imagining my spirit as a multifaceted diamond; when all the facets are clear, then the diamond gleams beautifully and gives off light; when some facets are covered by dirt, there is little light, little awareness. I sense losing my spark when I have lost connection to the sacred.

I began attending the Unitarian Church in Schenectady the year I received an appointment to Union College. I invited Rev. Bill Gold, the minister of this church, to one of my classes. What prompted this invitation was remembering that one of my favorite writer-philosophers, Ralph Waldo Emerson, was once a Unitarian minister. Reverend Gold's straightforward responses to questions about spiritual life drew my interest; his knowledge of world religions drew my respect. I was quickly drawn to this liberal religion, with its viewpoint that seemed free of dogma.

I knew that in Unitarianism, I had finally found a religious credo I could embrace. I could embrace a religion that urged children to learn about all the great world religions before making a decision. I could embrace a religion that was dedicated to social service. I could embrace a religion that began each service with this bond of union:

"Love is the spirit of this church,
The quest for truth is its sacrament,
And service is its prayer.
To dwell together in peace,
To seek knowledge in fellowship,
That all may grow in harmony with the good,
Thus do we covenant with one another."

I am willing to trust a belief system that includes both pagan and Christian teachings along with the wisdom layered in the philosophies of East and West. The Winter Solstice and Christmas are both rituals worth celebrating. The Buddha and Jesus Christ are both wise teachers.

It was at one Sunday service while in the throes of trying to find a title for my autobiography that I had an *eureka!* experience. The hymn we turned to was *Let It Be A Dance.* I almost blurted outloud, "That's it! Let It Be A Dance. Let Life Be A Dance. Let My Life Be A Dance!"

If, indeed, life is like a dance, what has this art and vital form of recreation taught me? M.C. Richards reminds us that "All the arts we practice are an apprenticeship. The big art is life." Here are some observations related to social dancing that have helped me better understand myself and others.

Upon greeting a colleague or friend I have not seen for some time, the first question they ask is, "Are you still dancing?" They seem buoyed up by my positive reply. Could it be that their inquiry masks a secret desire? I have a sneaking suspicion that every man would like to dance like Fred Astaire and, in fantasy, is just waiting for the opportunity to jump out of a telephone booth, not in a Superman costume, but in his "white tie and tails." I also suspect that every woman longs to be Ginger Rogers, spinning around a ballroom in her stunning gown, dancing with Fred.

The cliche, "It takes two to tango," applies off, as well as on, the dance floor. Passion, grace, improvisation and variety are characteristics of elegant dancers, enviable in any relationship. Being a couple requires much skill. So does dancing. There can't be a possessive clutch or a heavy hand. Of course, there is an old Greek proverb that says, "Dance alone and you can jump all you wish." But who wants to dance alone?

In the role of leader on the dance floor, I need to communicate with my partner and let her know where I want her to go. It's like driving; only one person can be at the wheel. But the role of following is hardly a passive one. When the follower is going forward, it is she who supplies the momentum. It took me some time to realize that I did not need to do all the work, that if I clear the path I can go along for a free ride. I have been trying to follow this rule off the dance floor as well.

Communication between partners on the dance floor is non-verbal—the way I position and move my body signals my intent. Off the dance floor, however, I use words to let my partner know my thoughts and feelings. I realize how much more adept I am at communicating with words than through movement. I wonder how much more eloquent we might be had we given more attention to learning the language of the body.

It seems to me a paradox that through dancing I have experienced the best of times and the worst of times. Going dancing with my wife is a source of great pleasure. When my body began breaking down, necessitating a back fusion and hip replacements, we could not always attend dances or take lessons together. It took my wife the better part of a year to act upon her strong need to go dancing and to take lessons on her own. Before I could accept this change, when she did go to dances alone or take lessons without me, I felt abandoned. I was apprehensive that she might meet someone whom she preferred as a partner both on *and* off the dance floor.

My initial reactions were self-centered and prompted by my insecurity. I had to realize that trust was at the core of our relationship and that each of us has vital needs which must be honored if the relationship is to flourish. Buber said, "In loving bondage free."

My wife became my dance partner but also my partner for life. Dancing allows us to hold or be held by other partners on the dance floor, without undue fear that these momentary embraces will land us in divorce court. Having more than one dance partner lends variety and spice to both our lives. We need to be alert to the demon jealousy, always ready to rear its ugly head. Demons take many forms and seem to be everywhere. You can spot a demon in a dance studio when one partner approaches the teacher and says of their mate: "Fix him!" or "Fix her!"

Dancing is a public act, as is living. We like to watch couples on the dance floor and, if we have some skill, like to be watched in return. It embarrasses us to find out that we are on *Candid Camera*, yet, in our lives we are always on *Candid Camera*. Perhaps, it is just as well not to dwell on this observation for we might become self-conscious, and like the centipede, would not know which of our legs to move first. I am glad to have only two legs to worry about.

What chutzpa to walk out on the tennis court or golf course never having received any instruction! Yet, all too many assume that if you can walk, you can dance. Wrong! Just as with any other sport, you have to work at it.

Being a teacher, I could not help but to include this pop quiz about dancing and life.

"How do you avoid bumping into other couples, on and off the dance floor?"

"How do you not hinder nor encumber your partners in their movements?"

"How do you keep the rhythm and improvise in a spirit of free play?"

Growing up, there were times I almost lost the flavor of the dances my parents danced, wanting only to do American "square dances." Through my parents, I have maintained a strong connection to my European heritage, a heritage rich in melody. Through my marriage to a Latin-American, I have also developed a strong connection to Latin-American dances, with their rich contribution of complex rhythms. Both streams, melody and rhythm, flow together and nourish my soul.

At the core of dancing is keeping the rhythm, the regular beat coming over and over in harmonious relationships. I do not find it difficult to keep to the rhythm in the waltz and the foxtrot; the down-beat of each musical phrase is accented. In dances like the rumba and the mambo, however, the rhythms are more irregular and complex. In the Latin-American dances, I begin on the unaccented, up-beat of a musical phrase. In these dances, I find it more difficult to know when to begin and how to keep to the syncopated beat.

It is easier to keep to the rhythm in my life when it has a regular beat, like my heart beat. Following the down-beat, I feel there is order in my life and that I am in control. I live by clock time. It is more challenging to keep the rhythm in my life when it does not have a regular beat. Suddenly confronted with unexpected and unplanned events, I must be spontaneous and improvise. Whether dancing on the down-beat or the up-beat, I heed the advice of jazz musicians: "Stay in the groove!"

If you ask me what my favorite ballroom dance is, I will reply, "The dance I am doing." But should you press me, I will answer, "The Argentine Tango." When I dance this dance, I get in touch with being a male and I simulate a macho attitude on the dance floor. The Argentine Tango, with its pulsating rhythms and exotic melodies, strikes a chord deep inside me. Perhaps, the affinity I feel toward this dance has something to do with the fact that, at the time the tango was evolving in Buenos Aires, forty percent of the population were immigrants from Italy.

Two natural partners are music and dance. As the music, so the dance. When I hear popular music, if I can't keep my body from moving, or my foot from tapping, it is dance music. And when my wife and I tune into music which excites us, we exchange knowing glances and can't help but want to dance together. Being crafty, if I want to hurry a meal my wife is preparing, I put on lively music and dinner appears presto. If I want to signal my amorous intent, I put on romantic music. I realize this is blatant manipulation, but what the hell?

Perhaps I *am* getting old, for I must acknowledge that, compared to dancing, sex is over-rated. Life, like dancing, is more than heavy breathing. The richness of life is more fully reflected in what can happen on the dance floor than in bed. Each dance (and there are hundreds of folk dances and scores of ballroom dances) has a unique rhythm pattern and feeling which energizes parts of the body besides those below the belt.

My cousin Vinny respects tradition. In his youth, he learned the prevailing style of American dancing and perfected it. My inclination is to keep tracking the emerging style of International dancing. Honoring tradition, and being drawn to change, both work. Perhaps, making choices in life, as in dancing, is a matter of temperament.

I feel most alive when my life is smooth as a fox trot, exhilarating as a waltz, energetic as the lindy hop, lively as a samba, romantic as a rumba, bouncy as a meringue, racy as a quick step, pulsating as a mambo and passionate as a tango.

One final thought: As to the possibility that there is an afterlife, I go along with Woody Allen, whose view is: "I do not believe in an afterlife, although I am bringing a change of underwear." On the chance that there is a hereafter, I plan to take along an extra pair of dancing shoes just in case there's a big-band bash happening above or below.

ABOUT THE AUTHOR

Frank M. Calabria is Professor Emeritus of Psychology at Union College, a psychotherapist, and a long-time teacher and student of ballroom dancing. He is the author of *Dance of the Sleepwalkers: The Dance Marathon Fad*. He and his wife, Angela, live in Schenectady, New York, in the historic General Electric Realty Plot.